MW00679099

do you
want to go
to the mountain?

do you
want to go
to the mountain?

THE LIFE THAT WANTS GOD AND THE LIFE THAT GOD WANTS

THOMAS YOUNG

Published by Theology on Fire Publishing, Richmond, Texas.
Formatted by Anne McLaughlin, Blue Lake Design, Dickinson, Texas.
Cover design by Aaron McClung Design www.aaronmcclung.com

ISBN: 0-9774348-051599

This book is dedicated to my wife Erin. This book would not exist without you…nor would I be as happy as I am without you. You are simply one of God's most amazing works of art. Your love for God, your worship of Him in everyday life, and your servant's heart are unmatched. I see HIS fullness in you! I love you.

The Transfiguration

Six days later Jesus took with Him Peter and James and John his brother, and led them up on a high mountain by themselves. And He was transfigured before them; and His face shone like the sun, and His garments became as white as light. And behold, Moses and Elijah appeared to them, talking with Him.

Peter said to Jesus, "Lord, it is good for us to be here; if You wish, I will make three tabernacles here, one for You, and one for Moses, and one for Elijah."

While he was still speaking, a bright cloud overshadowed them, and behold, a voice out of the cloud said, "This is My beloved Son, with whom I am well-pleased; listen to Him!"

When the disciples heard this, they fell face down to the ground and were terrified. And Jesus came to them and touched them and said, "Get up, and do not be afraid." And lifting up their eyes, they saw no one except Jesus Himself alone.

—Matthew 17:1-8

Table of Contents

acknowledgements

To My Family

I thank God for my family. Each one of you has made a significant and meaningful contribution to my life. I just thank God for your lives. I want to give a special acknowledgement to Addie Lee James, my grandmother now with the Lord. She was used by God to touch my life and help me along the way. No words could express enough to explain my love and gratefulness to God for her.

My children: Morgan, Graham, and Claudia. You are simply the greatest children on the planet. I cannot wait to see how God is going

9

to use your lives. You are His missionaries. My dad "PePops," you are proof God is real. Mom, thanks for always loving me. Uncle Bill, coming to my games and being my soccer coach meant more to me than you will ever know. Grandma Elaine, thanks for giving me Erin! Jo Jo and Ritchie, Eric, Melissa, Ash and Addie, you all are awesome in-laws, and not every says that…you are awesome!

To Our Board of Directors
of Young Endeavors Inc.,
The Ministry with Thomas Young

K.D. and Becky Moore, You are great friends and phenomenal people. You have no idea how much it means to us that you believe in us. You are simply a jewel of support and encouragement. You are just incredible to us. You often blow us away.

Frank and Bobbie Hood, You are remarkable friends. Coming over to your house to fellowship is something we treasure. How you invest in us is a blessing beyond measure. We count you everyday as one of the biggest blessings in our journey. You are always there for us…we need you.

Jerry and Cindy Pfister, You are fantastic friends and simply an unbelievable resource of wisdom. To us and the world, you are invaluable proof that you can have a godly family in this world today. Our gratitude for how you invest in us cannot be adequately expressed. We are grateful to you for your support and so much more.

Joe and Nancy Gilliam, God put us together many years ago. I was a 20 year-old punk who sensed that God called to preach, and God has used you to mold me to what He desires. What you have invested in me and this ministry is priceless.

Cynthia Coffman, my assistant, you are just out of this world! Your God-given ability to manage the ministry of Young Endeavors and my speaking schedule is unmatched. You are a gift from God we value beyond words. You are the best.

To Friends

Kelly and Beth Green: You believed when seemingly no one else did. You have made and are making a huge deposit in our lives. I owe you more than a greeting in a book! Joel and Valerie Engle: Joel, my college roommate and best friend. I would die for you. Besides my wife, no single individual has been used more powerfully by God to change my life than you. You are anointed and lead worship like no one else I know. And Val, you are unbelievable. The most grace dispersing person I have ever met. Mark and Amy Aduddell, We love you as the closest of friends. You are always there believing in us and praying for us. We treasure our times together and we always feel refreshed being around you both. Our kids adore you and your family. So do we.

Greg and Mary Clark, Greg you are our life long pastor. You and Mary are one of the brightest spots in my yearly travels. Coming to your house is like suddenly being treated as though I have become one of the most important people in the world. (not true of course) Your care for me is needed and appreciated more than you know. I love you and your church. Aaron and Jamie Ivey, we love you and it is incredible when I am speaking and your band (Spur 58) is leading worship! Bob and Nedra Funk, It's been a while but I am here doing what I do today in the blessing of the Lord because you took the time to pay attention to me. When I needed it most during many turbulent years of youth… you invested. I cannot thank you enough. Rod and Linda Masteller, you just don't know how a short period of time with you both helped Erin and I. Diane (you told me and showed me the gospel). "Thanks" doesn't get it on this one!

To More Friends and Ministry Partners

Thanks to all of you!

Ken and Linda Rivet, Winn and Lonni Pat Holloway, Matt and Julie Kearns, Scott and Kim Kindig (Simply a stunning leader and now a pastor), Doug Couch (and the GA Baptist Convention), Chad Childress (NAMB), Jason and Nan Britt, Quart and Carrie Graves (Thanks for the ranch house so I could write this book), Spur 58 (Bush, Kadar, Jimmie, and Chadwick), Jason Elam Band (Teasley, Topher, and Bishop), Charlie Hall and Nathan and Christie Knockels (still the best camp ever!), Bryan and Christie Gilmore, John and Mary Kay Neidhamer (You're our Florida-sized blessing from God), Mark and Leilani Morris, Liz Hunt, Victor and Ester Flores and the Bell Shoals Baptist Church, Simeon and Beth Nix, Robert and Beth Menchaka,

Dr. Mack Roark (Thank you for making the study of Greek a lifetime task), Dr. Roy Fish at Southwestern Baptist Theological Seminary, Tom and Christine DeLay, Ken and Pam Munday, Pastor Ken and Renata Galyean of Brindlee Mountain (Uganda will never be the same), Pastor Allan Blume and the wonderful Mt. Vernon BC of Boone, NC, Jim Lehew and Mike Booth (Emmaus!), James Lankford at the BGCO, Matt and Rachel Setliffe, Stuart and Terra Henslee, Luke and Carla Kaskey, Julius and Eloise Zatopek, Kent and Shawna Shingleton and the TBC, Kyle and Amy Goen (FBC Smyrna rocks), R: 81 (Gabe, Shane, and Neil—you are more than a band!), Pastor John Cross (South Biscayne is a phenomenal church), Pastor David Uth at FBC Orlando, Pastor Ed Emmerling (I love Michigan because of you), Valley Bakersfield (a Lighthouse in California!), Pastor Henry Severri and Mary (we love Africa because of you), Pastor Jay and Karen McFadden of IBC Stuttgart, Germany (and we love Germany because of you), Steffen Kahl (you rock Germany), Worship Pastor Ken Hartley, Pastor Steve and Karen Cochran (Macedonia, thank you!), Norma Bagley, Kyle and Darla Luttrell (dude I am proud of you), Coach Bob and Kelli Hoffman (Boomer Sooner), Chris and Heather Estes.

Thanks to Pat Springle of Baxter Press

Pat, thank you for all your insight, expertise, skill, and obvious love for communicating God's Word to the world. Your help in preparing this book is invaluable. I'm deeply grateful to you and the Lord for all your hard work in helping me with this book. I could not have done it without you.

For more information contact Pat Springle at www.baxterpress.com.

introduction

(Read this before you begin!)

Life is a mission trip.

This sentence has had a profound impact on me. As I travel and speak each week, I've quoted this statement to thousands of people. I'm convinced that a lot of Christians are missing out on God's best—not for a lack of effort, but because they lack "enoughness." Some would say they don't have enough of Christ, but that's not the problem. In reality, God doesn't have enough of them.

For many of us—maybe you—there's a missing link. We exert a lot of effort and even put a strong emphasis on God in our lives. However, there are many occasions in our thoughts and actions where God is perceived as a part of life but not life itself. He's *most* things, *a lot of* things, and a *great* thing, but not everything. Many of us simply aren't experiencing the "all" of the Christian life because we've segmented our lives into different duties performed at different times. We try hard to make each part work well, but we miss a cohesive, all-encompassing purpose.

God, then, becomes just one of the segments. Some of us carve out an hour on Sunday mornings, and we feel satisfied as we check off this week's commitment to spiritual life (especially if we felt warm or excited during that hour). Others add a segment of time for a small group or daily devotions. When we walk out the door or close our Bibles, we feel sure we've done "the God thing." We hear people talking about walking with God all day every day, but that seems like a pipe dream—too distant, too mysterious, and too difficult. We simply can't imagine making every moment of every day a God segment. That would take up our whole day!

Segmentation may make sense for math equations and engineering problems, but life is about relationships. God doesn't want to be scheduled in our PDAs for an hour here and an hour there. He is the Creator and Sustainer. In Him all things hold together. Apart from Him, we can do nothing. We desperately need His wisdom and power in every conversation, every task, and every plan. God doesn't want to just help us along our journey every now and then like a traffic cop directing us through a confusing intersection. God is the journey. Knowing and loving Him is the biggest adventure life offers on the planet. Everything else is part of the scenery along the way.

The answer isn't to worship more intensely or pray harder during a designated, segmented hour. The answer is to radically change our perspective about life, to see God as the air we breathe and the path we walk. Then and only then will we learn to walk in the fullness of what we already have in God, and we'll be satisfied in Him. This change in our perspective brings us the greatest thrills and the biggest challenges life can offer.

Some of us think that a life fully devoted to Christ requires only stern, grim decisions. The Bible uses language like "denying ourselves," "taking up our cross," and "being crucified with Christ." These actions are indeed a part of the journey as we follow Christ, and we must give them our attention. However, they are not the satisfaction and substance of the Christian life in and of themselves. Merely keeping the rules and regulations can cause us to be driven away from enjoying God and experiencing the "all" in our walk with God.

Author and pastor John Piper comments, "When we see Jesus for who he really is, we savor him. That is, we delight in him as true and beautiful and satisfying. . . . Christ is most glorified in us when we are most satisfied in him. And when we are satisfied, we are crucified to the world."[1]

If you're like me, you have a hunger for more—much more—of God. I've had strong thoughts racing through my mind for years: "It's never enough! I want more!"

Haven't you? That may be why you're holding this book! My study of Jesus and His men on the mountain at the transfiguration was life changing for me. Let me warn you. If God works in your heart like He did in mine through these eight verses in Matthew 17, you'll be gripped with the significance of God's glory like never before. Probably the most important thing God taught me is that the Christian life isn't about me; it's about Him. Far too often I've focused on *my* growth, *my* service, *my* success as a Christian, but that focus is off base. The central purpose of the universe is to bring honor and glory to the God who created it, and the central purpose of your life and mine is the same thing: to bring honor and glory to the one who created us, ransomed us from hell, and gave us real life.

The Scriptures have incredible power. They cut into the deepest recesses of our hearts and expose our hidden hopes and fears. They correct us when we fail and encourage us to value the things God treasures. The message of this book is rooted in a single passage, a particular event in the life of Jesus Christ, who was God in the flesh, walking the earth. We look to the Word of God as our guide because "the Scriptures alone are our vineyard in which we all ought to work and toil!"[2]

God's message to me from the mountain where Christ was transfigured was a revelation that smashed into my exhausted world. I had been traveling from city to city, preaching and pouring out my heart.

I felt as though most of my messages were sermons begging Christians to just "get with it"! I was telling people—no, I was so frustrated I was shouting at the top of my lungs—to "just do it"! I even told them one of my favorite statements from Martin Luther (one of my heroes of the faith) who said, "Let God be God!" I guess I hoped people would think my anger was righteous indignation, but it wasn't. It was just the fuming of frustration.

I was promoting "radical Christian living" with fierce intensity, and it was draining the life out of me. It was far too much about me—my vision, my purposes, and my efforts to change lives. It wasn't enough about God. I felt like I was drowning. I was being pulled in and sucked under the current instead of riding on the wave of God's love and power. In a moment of clarity, I wondered, *How can this happen to someone traveling all over the world preaching God's Word?*

I saw obvious and tragic needs in the world, and I saw puny, ineffective efforts made by the church to respond to them. My desire was to try to make people do what they ought to do—or at least, what *I thought* they ought to do. Instead of inviting them to be God's partners in the most exciting, thrilling, satisfying journey they could imagine, I tried to force them to work harder, serve more, and be more passionate. I urged them: "You ought to witness to unbelievers, read your Bible, pray harder, give far more, memorize Scripture, and go to church every time the doors are open! We've got to get off the sideline and get on the frontline!" Boy, I thought I was doing a great job telling all those people (or I should say *victims)* what they needed to do.

You can imagine the reactions I got. A few people patted me on the back and cocked their heads as if to say, "Go get 'em, Thomas!" But most people hit the doors as soon as the last "Amen" was spoken. I don't blame them. To be honest, I felt exactly the same way. I'd been working harder and doing more, and I was worn out. I was tired and discouraged. My pursuit of more only left me feeling I had less to give. I asked myself, *How could I be doing so much and feeling so empty? What's missing? What's wrong? How can I bring some life and hope back to my heart? Surely there's a better way.*

IN THE MIDST OF ALL MY FRANTIC ACTIVITY AND GUILT-RIDDEN MESSAGES, A GRACIOUS GOD GAVE ME A REVELATION OF HIMSELF.

It was a moment I'll never forget. He took me to Matthew 17, and I spent hours devouring the first eight verses. They were light and salt to me. After a while, I tried to read other passages, but I couldn't. God kept drawing me back to this passage like iron to a magnet. In this account—a single event in Jesus' life—I found wisdom and rest. Through these verses, God opened the eyes of my heart and gave me a fresh, powerful perspective that shocked me into a new reality of love for Him.

As days passed, God wouldn't let me leave the mountain with Jesus and His men because He wanted to use that event to change my life forever. He was going to take me from the performance trap to the partaking of triumph! He was going to teach me that "being" precedes "doing." I had heard those terms for years, but obviously, they hadn't sunk into my thick skull (and my thick heart). I was finally learning that God is far more excited about my knowing and loving Him than burning myself out with frantic activity for Him. Out of the overflow of that all-encompassing, incredibly rich relationship, I would be willing—no, I would be thrilled—to do whatever He wanted me to do. Guilt-motivation would be washed away in the flood of forgiveness, love, and acceptance. And then I would be able to share that powerfully attractive message with others instead of bludgeoning them with guilt. (And all the people said, "Amen, Thomas!")

I kept reading, studying, thinking, contemplating, and searching the treasures of truth in Matthew 17:1-8. I found that life and ministry are all about God's glory. To be honest, most of us don't understand much about the glory of God. We've sung about it for years, and we've heard preachers talk about it dozens of time, yet it hasn't gripped our hearts. But on the mountain that day with Jesus, the men with Him saw, heard, and felt the awesome glory of God—and they were never the same. Grasping the importance of God's glory is life changing. It's the foundation of an accurate view of God. The glory of God is all around us in creation, and it is demonstrated most powerfully by the Almighty, infinite God becoming flesh and blood so He could relate to us. As we bask in the wonder of God's glory, we reflect His nature, His love, and His compassion.

Experiencing the joy and wonder of the glory of God is a journey. In fact, it's life's ultimate journey. I'm not sure why I missed it for so long, but I'm so glad God broke into my emptiness and filled it with hope. Can you relate? Do you long to experience more of God? If you're like I was before God touched my life so dramatically, you can give some theological platitudes about the glory of God, but it may not make much of a dent in your everyday life. You may have put God in a few segments of your week, but in your heart, you know that's not enough. You've tried hard to be the person God wants you to be. You've confessed sin and you've gotten involved in helping people. But as author Randy Alcorn observed, "The Christian life is far more than sin management. Behavior modification that's not empowered by God's heart changing grace is self-righteous, as repugnant to God as the worst sins people gossip about."[3]

If you sense that something is missing in your life . . . if you are one of the many who are on a passionate pursuit to know God . . . if you are someone who is hungry for a "head-" and "heart-" changing journey with Him . . . then I invite you to come to the mountain with me. There, we will be transformed by God and catapulted into the greatest life we could ever know. Come on, let's go to the mountain.

"SIX DAYS later . . ."

1

I stick my finger

in carbonated drinks.

That sounds disgusting, doesn't it? Sorry about that. Why do I stick my finger in carbonated drinks? Because I discovered that the sodium and other chemicals in my skin cause the fizz to disperse really quickly, and I don't have to wait for the fizz to go down so I can finish filling the cup! Efficiency is a good thing, but this kind of impatience can drive you (and those around you) nuts!

God is interested in every moment of your life, the good times and the bad. Impatience is a product of misplaced priorities. For most of us who experience it, impatience is the product of thinking we'll somehow have more success and approval if we get more done faster. God wants us to experience every single moment as a gift from Him and a source of joy . . . or a lesson. Even while waiting for the fizz to go down, I can use the time to remember that God is the source of my hope instead of rushing to get more done more quickly. Most of us don't learn this lesson very easily.

Walter Ciszek gained this perspective in one of the most heart-wrenching stories I've ever heard. Ciszek felt led by God to be a minister in Russia, but his board sent him instead to Poland. When the Nazis invaded Poland in 1939 and the borders with Russia suddenly opened, Ciszek thought his prayers were answered. He slipped across the border, but he was soon captured, arrested as a spy, and sent to a Soviet prison. He suffered for five years in solitary confinement, then spent many more in a harsh gulag. During that time, God worked deeply in Ciszek's heart. He was tempted to become bitter and wallow in self-pity, but God gave him patience and wisdom. In his book, *He Leadeth Me,* Ciszek reflected, "Each day to me should be more than an obstacle to be gotten over, a span of time to be endured, a sequence of hours to be survived. For me, each day came forth from the hand of God newly created and alive with opportunities to do his will. . . . Between God and the individual soul, there are no insignificant moments; this is the mystery of divine providence."[4]

If we view time as a hindrance as we rush to the next item on our agenda, we will miss precious moments to behold the wonder of God along the way.

The story in Matthew 17:1-8 is about Jesus inviting Peter, James, and John to go to the mountain with Him. He's still inviting people. He invited me, and He's inviting you. The day I started devouring this passage, I sensed the Holy Spirit tapping me on the shoulder and whispering, "Thomas, do you want to go to the mountain?" Long hikes take some time, and they require some patience. If we hurry, we'll miss some of what God wants for us.

Do you want to go to the mountain? If you do, let's go.

Matthew 17:1 says, "Six days later Jesus took with Him Peter and James and John his brother, and led them up to a high mountain by themselves."

The day I started reading this passage, I had my journal and my Bible in my lap. As I read, every word was pregnant with meaning. The first words were, "Six days later. . . ." These are words that would normally cause me to want to "stick my finger in the fizz" to speed up the process of learning. But Matthew recorded this pause in the life of Jesus for a reason. Do you get it? He's telling us that something took a long time.

We may be able to rush bank transactions and fast food orders in drive-thru lanes, and we may be able to cook a full meal in sixty seconds with a microwave, but spiritual growth takes a bit longer than that! If we try to stick our fingers in the fizz of our spiritual lives, our impatience will short-circuit some of what God wants to teach us. I've heard pastor and author Chuck Swindoll say that waiting is the hardest task for us today. I agree! But waiting forces us to slow our minds, focus our hearts, and become alert to the whisper of God's Spirit. We don't get that by rushing through life.

The phrase "six days later" is an important introduction to Matthew's account of the transfiguration of Jesus. It's like a warning light on the dash of a car. The lights send us a message that something important is happening: the oil pressure is low, we're running out of gas, or we need to find a mechanic. The span of six days at this point in Jesus' life separates a public event from a private one. Matthew's words flash a message to us that we'd better pay attention because something very important is going to happen.

Six days before this moment, Jesus and all of His followers were on a hillside near the Sea of Galilee. Thousands of people had seen Jesus heal the lame and give sight to the blind. They were amazed! But they had forgotten something . . . lunch. Jesus had compassion on them, and He miraculously fed them. The passage says that four thousand were fed that day, but that's only the men. Including women and children, probably twelve to fifteen thousand people got a free lunch from Jesus that afternoon.

The point is not that God is interested in Happy Meals. Rather, God wanted to validate the message of forgiveness by performing miracles. It was a corporate experience of the wonder of God. These dramatic acts revealed to the world that Jesus is the Messiah. A few days later, though, God had a different agenda. Instead of a public display, Christ reserved a special demonstration of His wonders for three of His closest followers. The public display was for the world; the private one was for worshipers. Public, miraculous demonstrations of God's nature, character, and power are phenomenal to witness. But Jesus reserved a more wonderful demonstration for those who had left everything to follow Him. It was a moment with the few, not the masses. What God does to us, in us, and through us in private can have a greater impact on us that what He does in public. And then, as that love and power flow through us, we become more effective in reflecting His glory in public.

HOW MANY OF US ARE MISSING A LIFE FILLED WITH THE POWER OF GOD BECAUSE WE HAVE NEGLECTED EXPERIENCING HIS GLORY IN PRIVATE? GET THIS EMBEDDED INTO YOUR SPIRIT: WE NEED TO EXPERIENCE GOD IN PRIVATE TO BE MORE EFFECTIVE IN PUBLIC.

The power and wisdom we gain in private dictates how powerfully we are used in "public"! Our private, personal, and alone times with God will often precede a great and public work of God though us.

Do you desire with the utmost passion and intensity for God to use you to show the world His name and His glory? Then you must get past just going to church and awaiting the corporate presence of God. You need to go to the closet and await Him there! It will be during those moments alone in His presence that God changes us, and that experience will leave us undaunted! It's those private moments that solidify and amplify the rest of our lives. They seal us and make us stronger in our faith. Those moments move us from believing *in* God to *believing* God!

We can make two mistakes. One is to be satisfied with public displays of God's glory, trying to crank out the Christian life without absorbing God's love, forgiveness, and power during times of solitude with Him. Some of us go to worship service, sing the songs, hear the message, and we feel close to God—until just after lunch! Nothing permanent happens, and to be honest, we don't even know that more is available to us. We have a strange, nagging sense that there's more, but a lot of our friends don't even do what we do to connect with God. Compared to them, we're pretty radical in our commitment to Christ!

A second mistake lies at the other extreme. Far too many people are like I was: trying too hard to make things happen for God without enjoying a rich, loving relationship with Him. We can run on fumes for a little while, but soon, our tank is empty. We feel frustrated, angry that God isn't using us like He's using other people, and confused because trying really hard doesn't seem to be enough.

As I think back on my own experience during these dry times, I think of the chorus we often sing at church, "As the Deer Pants for the Water." It's a beautiful song, but I don't think many of us understand what the psalmist felt when he penned those words. The song is based on Psalm 42, a psalm of despair:

"As the deer pants for the water brooks,

So my soul pants for You, O God.

My soul thirsts for God, for the living God;

When shall I come and appear before God?

My tears have been my food day and night,

While they say to me all day long, "Where is your God?"

These things I remember and I pour out my soul within me."
(Psalm 42:1-4).

The deer wasn't prancing down by the stream, deciding to have a nice cool drink. No, it was dying of thirst! The psalmist was saying, "God, I'm dying here, and I desperately need You! In fact, I'm weeping because I miss You so much!"

I don't like pain any more than anybody else, but in my years of walking with God, I've noticed a pattern in myself and in many others: Most of us won't turn to God until and unless we feel desperate. We'll trust in our own intelligence, our skills, our ability to please people, and a hundred other things before we trust God. But God, in His mercy and grace, sooner or later brings us to the end of ourselves so that we see we have only one hope—Him. That moment isn't a tragedy. It's a glorious realization that God is worthy of our trust, our love, and our obedience. Nothing else counts. Nothing else matters. We then realize that trying to put on a public face of spirituality without privately knowing the God of grace is foolishness and hypocrisy.

Are you desperate for God?

I'm an avid reader, and I love to go to bookstores. I was walking through a bookstore years ago when I saw something that really bothered me. On the display shelf was a copy of *The One-Minute Bible*. One minute? In my barely masked cynicism that day, I thought about contacting the publisher with some similar book concepts. We could have *The One-Minute God, The Quick Spiritual Fix, Drive-Thru Jesus,* or *Get God and Go*. Yet that's typical of the way Christians approach God these days—a quick worship service (if it doesn't interfere with something else I'd like to do), a quick time of prayer (when I feel that I need something from God, my spiritual vending machine), or a quick time of reading the Bible (a minute here, a minute there).

The point is that one minute will not do! Yes, one minute or moment in God's Word can change your life, but our desire for "some" interaction must grow into a demand to experience "more"! Our desire for an encounter with God must bring us to the point of determining that our hearts will be spent in open exposure before God in private. There, we develop a desire for a radical life with God. This desire has to become unreserved, unhindered, and overt!

I want more than the typical, "catch God and run" connection. I long for a phenomenal relationship with God! Again, one minute just won't do. Isaiah wrote, "Those who wait for the Lord will gain new strength" (Isaiah 40:31). The psalmists longed to be in the presence of God. Paul expressed the same sentiment. He wanted his readers to know what he had discovered: "the love of Christ which surpasses knowledge" (Ephesians 3:19). Our fast-paced, instant-answer culture promises that we can get whatever we want in a heartbeat, but that's not true. To touch the heart of God—and better yet, to have Him touch our hearts—requires focus, attention, longing, hope, and time. It simply can't be rushed.

When Jesus miraculously fed the four thousand, wouldn't it have been nice if everyone could have stayed together eating the bread and fish as one big happy family? But the Christian life is not about sitting and watching Jesus supply us with an endless supply of physical gifts. It's about valuing the unseen more than the seen, stocking up treasures in heaven, and wanting to experience God's heart more than anything else in the world. We have to go beyond *public, natural* feeding to discover *private, supernatural* feasting with God. We need to find moments with Him in private that will give us passion for Him and Him alone. The irony is that as we pursue God, we find more satisfaction than we ever dreamed, but we thirst for even more.

Please don't misunderstand. I'm not against public worship, concerts, and things like that. Not at all! But I want to say as clearly as possible that these public events are not all there is. Jesus is happy to show Himself to the masses, and those experiences are wonderful and meaningful. But He longs to take us up the mountain, to be alone with us so He can share His glory with us in a private setting. There, we can go beyond the usual to the phenomenal, from seeing Christ at a distance to hearing Him whisper our names, from enjoying physical blessings He gives us to learning the secrets God has hidden for those who truly seek Him.

Is your heart stirring with a longing, a passion for more? Do you really want God to touch your life? No, that's not a trick question, and the answer may not be as obvious as you think. Many of us would rather stay at arm's length from Christ. Getting too close to the fire is risky. But others feel a longing deep in their bones to experience more of Christ. I think it's perfectly right to ask God for an obsession to know Him better. He wants to be far more than our hobby, and I think He delights to hear us ask Him to make knowing Him the consuming passion of our lives. He must become our phenomenon.

We need our hearts and heads to be affected by God. This can and does happen corporately. However, it is during quiet moments with Him after the huge "meeting of feeding" that we can plunge past the normalcy that sometimes follows such a meeting and enjoy the propelling power of God manifested in us through an encounter with Him alone!

If we're serious about knowing Jesus more deeply, what can we expect? That's a hard one. There aren't any simple, blanket answers. A casual reading of the stories of men and women in the Bible shows that

God uses a wide variety of personalities in phenomenal ways. Some became kings; some became martyrs. Some lived quiet lives of faithful service; others had a passion that flamed for all to see. I certainly can't predict what God's plan is for you, but I can promise you this: It'll be an adventure!

A few people who have read this far may be convinced this isn't for them. They're headed to the bookstore right now to get their money back! But because I've talked to thousands of men and women, young and old, about going to the mountain with Jesus to see His glory, I'm convinced that most of us are ready to lace up our sandals and hit the trail.

"Great, now what?" (Isn't that what we say when we're hammered by the Holy Spirit and convicted that our lives fall short?) What are some things that foster this pursuit of Christ in private encounters? God has provided some "tools" for us to use in applying the truths we'll examine together. Let me highlight three of them for you.

Intentional Solitude to Hear

It may sound strange, but there's a distinct sound in solitude. It's very important for us to be so quiet that we are aware of the absence of sound. How often does that happen these days? We are a plugged-in generation, and we have very few moments during our day when sound isn't pressing in on us. It's exceptionally difficult to listen to the Spirit when we're being bombarded by all kinds of noise. So find a place and a time that is so quiet that you become aware of the absence of sound. Then you'll be able to concentrate, and you can hear the whisper of the Spirit's voice.

I need to warn you, though, that you'll experience distractions. In fact, I guarantee it. One of the devil's favorite tactics is to promote busyness and create distractions (in our homes, with our families, at our work, and in our thoughts) so we can't enjoy the solitude we need in order to maintain the presence of God.

Purposeful Contemplation to See.

We will continue to find it difficult to "see" God and what He is doing unless our hearts and minds are attuned to seeing Him. Sometimes I find a quiet place, open my Bible, and lay out my journal. I'm ready to go! But after a while, nothing has dented my cranium. For me, the reason I sometimes don't get much out of my time of reflection is that I'm not really reflecting at all. I'm just reading. Have you ever read a few pages of a novel, then somebody asked, "Hey, what are you reading?" and you couldn't think of what you just read? That sometimes happens to me even when I'm reading the Bible. That kind of absentmindedness isn't quite worthless, but it's close!

I need to prepare my heart for reflection, so I pray first: "God, thank You for meeting with me right now. I trust Your Spirit will guide me and teach me. I want to follow You, Lord. Give me ears to hear and courage to act on what You say to me today." That prayer focuses my heart and my mind, and I then expect God to answer my prayer.

Treasure the Word to Know

I have some terrific friends who get excited when they open God's Word because they fully expect God to use it in their lives. They really believe that the words on those pages have been sent to them by God Himself, to teach them about His character, show them how to live the most exciting life in the world, keep them from getting off track, and get them back on track when they blow it. These friends treasure the Bible, and they are constantly learning more about God's truth. They have a wonderful blend of certainty and wonder, and their lives reflect both. As they study, they learn more and more about God's purposes, yet also come to realize that they have a long way to go in plumbing the depths of the mysteries of God!

My friends soak their minds in the truth of God's Word, and I have to tell you, they are the most attractive people I know. But please understand, these people are treasure hunters. They invest time and energy into their understanding of the Scriptures because they're convinced that the jewels they find are well worth the effort. They fervently devour God's truth as if they were eating food after a week without it. That's what meditation is all about: filling our minds with truth so the Spirit of God can transform our hearts and our behavior.

We must learn to meditate to fuel the learning curve of our life! We must remain undaunted as we chew on the meaning of the words of God after reading them in our daily private moments before Him.

> ## The Word of God is taught as it is thought.

Christian meditation isn't just stopping all thought activity of the mind. In his wonderful book, *Celebration of Discipline,* Richard Foster observed, "Eastern meditation is an attempt to empty the mind; Christian meditation is an attempt to fill the mind."[5]

An ancient proverb applies to our study of God's Word: "Whatever you starve dies and whatever you feed grows!" Meditate, feast, and soak your mind in God, His Word, His nature, His character, and His creation like never before. God will meet you and change your life.

"Six days later. . . ." These words mean something happened a few days ago, and something important is coming. Isn't that why you're reading this book? Do you want to go to the mountain? That's where we're headed. Come on!

Note: Reading books is of great value to stimulate thinking and teach us principles, but I've found that pointed questions and exercises help me apply those principles more specifically to my own life. Perhaps you will, too. At the end of each chapter, you'll find a section titled "Think about it." Use the questions and exercises to reflect, pray, and consider how God might want to shape your attitudes and actions so you will become more fully devoted to Him.

Think about it . . .

1. What are some of the symptoms of "hurry sickness," being rushed all the time? What are some reasons people are in such a hurry? Are you in a hurry a lot of the time? Explain your answer.

2. Think about this statement: "We can make two mistakes: We can be satisfied with the public displays of God's glory, and we can try to crank out the Christian life without soaking in God's love, forgiveness, and power in times of solitude with Him." Do either of these mistakes affect your life? If not, why not? If so, what can you do about it?

3. Read Psalm 42:1-4, and then read it again. Can you point to a time when this prayer expressed your heart's desire? Describe that time. Is it your desire now?

4. Review the last section of practical suggestions to get more out of your time alone with God. Which one stands out and is a priority for you? What will you do to take steps in that area?

NIGHT LIGHTS

FAIRY FLIGH

by

"JESUS took with Him . . ."

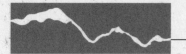

2

The mountain.

Jesus had a plan in mind. He knew exactly what He wanted to do, and He knew who He wanted to take with Him. After the public miracle, He wanted to share some private, intimate moments with three of His men. But He didn't want to have those moments just anywhere. He planned to take them to a mountain. It wasn't important which physical mountain it was. That wasn't the point. The mountaintop experience would be spiritual, not physical.

The mountain is where we witness and experience the glory of God, where we "taste and see that the Lord is good" (Psalm 34:8). It is where the experience of Him and the knowledge of Him collide and result in holy life change.

WE DON'T LIVE ON THE MOUNTAIN. IT'S A PLACE WHERE JESUS TAKES US.

The mountain is a place of reinvigoration, restoration, and revelation along the journey of life. There, those that seek Him with passion and reckless abandon see Him for who He is—and they are forever changed.

The words "Jesus took with Him" reveal a treasure to us. They indicate a wealth in the Christian life that we can enjoy and a potential for unbridled joy and exuberant passion. Comprehending this fact causes us to explode into a new walk of faith. You will never be the same again! These four words from Matthew 17:1 cut me like a knife. As I thought about the importance of the statement, "Jesus took with Him," I came face to face with my self-absorption. You see, I tend to think that I take Jesus with me! This single insight revolutionized my concept of myself, of God, and of the life He has offered me. Let me explain.

We live in a world of incredible advances in technology, medicine, economics, and every other field of science and business. In just the past fifty years, diseases have been eradicated that had once wiped out millions of people. New procedures in transplants, cancer treatments, surgical techniques, and medicines arrest death and bring a higher quality of life. The cost of all this progress is not just in higher health insurance bills. The real cost is in our hearts: We are tempted to believe that we don't need God any more. We now think we just need the latest medical procedure, the newest software, or a better investment technique to fix our problems and make us rich, good-looking, and happy. The concept of an almighty, omniscient God of wonder has been replaced by a heavenly Santa Claus whose goal is to meet our needs. Author and psychologist Larry Crabb observes that many of us think of God as "a specially attentive waiter."[6] When we get good service from Him, we thank Him with a nice tip of praise. When we don't get what we want, we gripe.

The apostle Paul was tough as nails. Luke's history of the early church tells us that Paul was one of the bravest, most tenacious leaders the church has ever known. Nothing could stop him! He endured beatings, shipwrecks, imprisonment, starvation, and all kinds of other abuse and privation. Paul makes a statement in his second letter to the Corinthian believers. He said, "But I am afraid." Afraid? Paul? When that guy says he's afraid, it gets my attention. His full statement was, "But I am afraid, lest as the serpent deceived Eve by his craftiness, your minds should be led astray from the simplicity and purity of devotion to Christ" (2 Cor. 11:3).

Paul saw the wealth and envy among the believers in Corinth, and he was alarmed! He warned them that they were valuing what was seen (possessions, positions, and popularity) more than the unseen (Christ,

God's Word, and the souls of men and women). This wrong perspective, he tells us, comes from the pit of hell, from Satan himself.

What would Paul say to you and me if he saw us today? I think he'd be just as afraid we would believe Satan's deceptions to value the wrong things . . . with disastrous results. Jesus is looking for people who fight the temptation to think that He exists for our benefit and that His value is only what He can do to make us happy. He's looking for people who see Him as their greatest treasure and gladly give up anything and everything to follow Him.

The statement "Jesus took with Him" has two important implications that powerfully contradict the idea that God is our attentive waiter. One is that Jesus calls the shots. He is sovereign and wise, and He knows what's best for His followers. He is, by definition of the word "Lord," our Master who commands our obedience by His powerful and loving nature. The second implication is that we grasp His sovereign right to lead us, and we gladly follow our Master. Paul wrote that we have been "bought with a price" by Christ's sacrifice on the cross for us. We are no longer our own. We are His.

For many people, the Christian journey is only about "getting saved" so they can make sure they go to heaven when they die. Their daily lives aren't touched by their faith much at all. Decisions about relationships, purchases, debt, purpose, and fun are made without a thought about God's will and ways. Church is a place to get their spiritual engines revved up a bit, but an hour or so later, they go back to "normal" and forget about God.

Several centuries ago, a pastor named Stephen Charnock, spoke and wrote about the excellencies of God and our response of wonder, worship, and obedience. Our current segmentation of life into a small pocket of spirituality and a far larger part of spiritual apathy isn't new. Charnock observed in his day, too, that many Christians lived as "practical atheists," forgetting about God most of the time as they made decisions about every aspect of their lives.

I often hear people talk about their faith and their lives as if the two are completely separate. Churches are somewhat to blame for this dichotomy. We categorize the Christian journey into various duties. We talk to people about evangelism, discipleship, and worship as if the Bible teaches that they're all separate. But for the believer, faith and life are inextricably meshed together. The truth of God and the Spirit of God guide us as we become increasingly aware of God's presence in us and in our circumstances all day every day. Gradually, we learn to see people from a new perspective (2 Cor. 5:16) and we understand that the realities of our circumstances are more unseen than seen (2 Cor. 4:16-18).

The verse at hand says, "Jesus took with Him. . . ." In my journey to the mountain, the revelation of this verse spoke volumes to my heart. I realized that real Christianity isn't about where we are taking Jesus, but where He is taking us. Do we have more authority than He does? He is the Creator of the vast universe of hundreds of billions of galaxies, and He knows the number of hairs on our heads. In Him, all things hold together. Are we wiser than God? He is the Alpha and the Omega, the beginning and the end, the one who knows everything about everything. We are puny, finite munchkins whose knowledge has increased a lot in the past few years, but the total of man's knowledge is a molecule in a drop in the vast ocean of God's infinite grasp of all things. Are we more powerful than God? God didn't sweat when He created the universe that is 14.6 billion miles across, yet I sweat when I fix a flat tire or run a lap around a track. We will be wise to think about our view of God. If we are honest, many of us will see that we believe God's job is to make us happy. So when we aren't happy, we too often complain about Him.

Jesus has the right to determine where He takes me, and I trust that His direction is always right. For much of my Christian life, I was terribly self-absorbed. I was more impressed with what I did for God than what He had done and is doing in me. I was more interested in people thinking I was wonderful than in thinking Jesus was wonderful. In ministry, I was glad for people to praise God . . . as long as they gave me credit for helping them trust in God. Perhaps we have to go through a stage when we're most excited about our abilities, our successes, and the way God is using us. But it's a pity if we stay there. God wants us to go deeper, and going deeper means that He must increase as we decrease.

Going deeper also means we grasp the fact that segmenting our lives won't cut it any more. God wants to be the Lord and Master of our fun with friends as well as our worship at church, of the boardroom and the bedroom, of our choices about movies and television, of our public face and our secrets hopes and fears. The Christian life is called a "walk" for good reason. Walking is slow, steady, persistent, and is often done with a companion. People who walk are far more aware of the bumps and the beauty along the path than those who drive by at 70 miles an hour or fly by at 30,000 feet.

We have some wonderful promises that Jesus is near to us on our journey.

He said, "I will never leave you nor forsake you," and "I am with you always." One of the names for Jesus is Emmanuel, "God with us." But we need to understand that if we're going to walk with Jesus, we need to choose all day every day to walk with Him and follow Him. If we choose to go a different way, our own way, we will experience the undesirable consequences of such a path. We can pout and demand that He should follow us, but He doesn't play those games. We can blame Him for not appearing to be right there with us (even though He is), but we need to change directions. Going to the mountain requires that we respond to His invitation. He "took [people] with Him."

Jesus Christ, our Savior, our Master, and our friend offers His hand and invites us to go with Him, but we have to understand that our path with Him will go where He leads us. Can we trust Him as our guide?

We often use words like "walking with Jesus" and "following Christ." These words can remind us that He is the wise guide who charts the path for us. Sometimes He takes us to the mountain of joy, but sometimes He takes us into the valley of suffering and trials.

Does God really take us into difficulties? Yes, He does. Struggles in our lives can be the result of our sins, others' sins against us, natural disasters, or any number of other causes. But even if they're caused by our own poor choices, we can see our struggles as God's instrument to chisel us to shape our character. In one of the most famous conversations in the Bible, Job's wife was furious at him for not being angry with God for all the disasters they had experienced: "Then his wife said to him, 'Do you still hold fast your integrity? Curse God and die!' But he said to her, 'You speak as one of the foolish women speaks. Shall we indeed accept good from God and not accept adversity?'" (Job 2:9-10)

Adversity in the valley is part of the journey. But in the account in Matthew 17, Jesus has a different agenda. He's taking three of His followers to the mountain. There, they'll have an experience that will change their perspective of Jesus.

As we see Jesus' outstretched hand inviting us to join Him, we need to remember that He is awesome in His power, wisdom, and love. We can trust Him with our painful pasts and our hopeful futures. We can take His hand and join Him on the journey. We may have some fears and doubts, but we still grab His hand and take a step down the path with Him.

Charles Spurgeon was one of the greatest Bible teachers in the history of our faith. He wrote, "The walk of faith is one protracted miracle. We see nothing beneath us or before us, yet we stand upon a rock and go from strength to strength."[7]

Do you sense Jesus reaching out His hand to you? He's going to the mountain. You and I can decide if we want to go with Him. I'm going. How about you?

Do you really want to go to the mountain?

Think about it...

1.   What are some ways you observe people treating God like He is "a specially attentive waiter"?

2.   What are some ways we can tell if we want to follow Christ or if we actually want Him to follow us?

3. Why is it important to have a richer, deeper grasp of the character of God as we consider whether to follow Him or not?

4. What fears do you have as you think of grasping Jesus' hand and going on the journey with Him? What hopes are in your heart?

"PETER, James, and John his brother . . ."

3

"This guy is drunk."

On the night before my wedding to my beautiful bride Erin, I was driving back to my apartment in the Dallas/Fort Worth Metroplex. We had just had our rehearsal dinner, and Erin had given me an engraved watch as a gift. I was getting married to the girl of my dreams, and life couldn't get any better. As I was driving, suddenly the car in front of me veered off of the highway, slid down an embankment, and flipped over on its top! In the light of my car's headlights, I saw the whole thing unfold.

I immediately stopped, jumped out of the car, and ran down the embankment. Since the car was upside down, the only way I could get to the driver was to crawl through the hole where the rear window used to be. The driver was suspended by his seat belt, and he was hanging upside down in his seat! I quickly crawled up next to him, and I began to talk to him. He was very disoriented, but I quickly discovered his foggy brain wasn't the result of the accident. He was drunk!

I've seen too many movie scenes of cars blowing up after an accident, so I quickly began removing the man from his car. All of his weight was pushed against the seat belt, and it was nearly impossible to push the button to release the belt. Finally, after wedging myself against him to push him away from the buckle, I got the belt to release. He fell in a clump, and I pulled him through the back window and out of the car. About this time, the police arrived with lights flashing and sirens blaring.

In situations like this, injured people shouldn't be moved unless it's absolutely necessary. Any movement increases the risk of making the injury worse. But I believed the man's life was more endangered by leaving him in the car than in moving him. I wanted to stay around and talk to the police, but I was getting married the next day. I quickly calculated that if I stayed, it would be hours before I got home. I didn't want to spend the rest of my evening answering questions and having someone take a statement, so I got in my car and drove away.

Since that night several years ago, I've often wondered how many times the man in the car told his story of the "angel" pulling him out of his car that night. I'm sure the police didn't believe him because he was so drunk, but they probably wondered how he got out of the car. None of them—the police, the drunk driver, or anyone else that arrived—knows that I was there. To them, I never existed.

Matthew's account tells us the names of the people Jesus chose to go with Him to the mountain. According to the record of the accident I witnessed, I had never been there. However, the presence of each person with Jesus on the mountain is on record. Matthew wrote, "Six days later Jesus took with Him Peter, James, and John his brother. . . ."

Hey, where were the other nine disciples? Where were the women who followed Him, and where was the crowd of people who seemed to hang around looking for lunch or other miracles? Of all the people who had been with Him just a few days before, Jesus only invited three of His guys to go with him. That bothered me. It *really* bothered me. Why only Peter, James, and John? He picked them. That's it . . . short and sweet. Jesus chose those three to accompany Him.

BUT THAT THOUGHT DIDN'T BOTHER ME NEARLY AS MUCH AS THE NEXT QUESTION THAT POPPED INTO MY MIND: WOULD HE HAVE PICKED ME?

To tell the truth, I felt despair because I couldn't honestly answer yes. In fact, I concluded the answer was: "I sure hope so!"

How would you answer that question?

No one likes to be left out. Everyone wants to be accepted. Our world is a competitive place. In business, sports, academics, and almost every other field of endeavor, the dreams of one are fulfilled while the ambitions of another are shattered. The question about being chosen by Jesus touches us at the very core of our souls. It terrifies us and challenges us. I believe the question is best seen as a challenge, not a condemnation.

What are Jesus' criteria for selecting us as His companions for the journey up the mountain? Is He looking for people with a deep knowledge of His Word? Is He searching for someone with unbridled passion to tell others about Him? Is He looking for people who spend hours with Him in prayer each day?

British philosopher and theologian, G. K. Chesterton, recognized that some truths in the Christian faith are seemingly incompatible. These include predestination and free will, God's awesome transcendence and His nearness. Chesterton called these "furious opposites," and he concluded that we are wise to keep them furious and keep them opposite so that our faith and our wonder grow.

In this passage, we find two furious opposites. We see that Jesus picked only three men from the twelve disciples (and dozens of others who may have been following Him, too). God had the right to make His sovereign choice. He chose Isaac and not Ishmael, and He chose

Jacob instead of Esau. One side of this furious opposite, then, is God's divine, sovereign, free choice to pick some of us—and not pick others. That's difficult for many of us to swallow. Yet the other "opposite" provides some balance and gives us encouragement.

We can make ourselves available to Jesus. I believe Christ is looking for people who are willing to reach out, take His hand, and take the next step down the road with Him. However, we must not get preoccupied with trying to figure out why God does what He does. In doing so we can miss the joy of each moment. It is far better to enjoy every encounter with Him, even when things don't completely make sense to us.

The issue is not about our questioning God's selection criteria. The real issue at hand is whether or not we make ourselves available and surrendered to Him. His first and foremost requirement is a responsive heart. Some of us will respond with a huge bear hug and all the enthusiasm of a puppy, but others hesitantly reach out an inch at a time, wondering what will happen if we reach all the way. Jesus was incredibly patient with Thomas when he doubted the resurrection, and He's just as patient with those of us who are timid today.

On the journey, Jesus is with us and has included us in His plan. He tells us about His creation and His plan for the future. He assures us that He knows exactly what He's doing, even when we don't have a clue. As we interact with Him along the way, our passion for Him is kindled or heightened, our trust in Him deepens, and our thirst for more grows stronger. Gradually, step by step as we hold His hand along the way, Jesus becomes all in all to us. And gradually, we take Him out of the segmented box of our "spiritual lives" and understand that He is to be worshiped in every part of our day and every choice we make.

To experience God in all of His fullness, we have to think right thoughts about Him. This is where some fall short in the Christian life. But again, Jesus is wonderfully patient to remind us who He is. After three years of being with Jesus day after day, you'd think the disciples would have a good idea what God was like. But they didn't. After the resurrection, two of them walked from Jerusalem to a little town called Emmaus (Luke 24:13-35). They were heartbroken because Jesus had been executed on the cross. Jesus, though, appeared to them, walked with them, and reminded them of everything the Bible said about Him. When He revealed Himself to them, they finally got it!

Our grasp of God's character comes from a growing understanding of the truth of God's Word. And as we grasp the love and power of His awesome character, we'll love Him even more. Author and speaker R. C. Sproul said, "To know Him is to love Him. Therefore, deepening knowledge must precede deepening affection."[8]

Knowing truth about God, though, isn't enough. That truth must be combined with trust in order to have an impact on our hearts and our behavior. The Christian life isn't just an academic exercise; it's a relationship with the most wonderful, most powerful, and most compassionate being in the universe. Our experience is based on God's truth, but it's energized by our childlike faith to take His hand and walk beside Him.

Author and pastor John Piper has written extensively about our desire to honor God. He wrote, "God is glorified in his people by the way we experience him, not merely by the way we think about him. Indeed the devil thinks more true thoughts about God in one day than a saint does in a lifetime, and God is not honored by it. The problem with the devil is not his theology, but with his desires."[9]

Do you want to go to the mountain? For us to go, Jesus has to pick us. But He doesn't choose us based on some arbitrary list of rules and restrictions. Our desire should be to go with Him to the mountain. We should be full of passion and aggressively pursue going with Him. He sees if we want to go with Him. Do we want to go?

Our flesh wants Jesus to make it easy. We want Him to pick us no matter what's in our hearts. God is looking for receptive, responsive hearts. But also, He has to pick us to go with Him. Does it bother you that you might not be picked? If so, that's good! Your concern shows you're on the right track. That humbling prick of hurt may cause you to seek Him like never before. You and I must become like the deer that pants for the water, longing and thirsting to know Him.

Are you sure you still want to go to the mountain?

Think about it...

1. Does it bother you that Jesus picked three of His disciples and not the others? Explain your answer.

2. What can we do to be ready?

3. Would Jesus pick you right now? Why or why not?

4. What are some things that inflame your desire to follow Jesus?

"and led them up on a
HIGH MOUNTAIN
by themselves . . ."

4

The Coiler.

That's the name of my new mountain bike. I'm a thrill-seeker. I love adventures, the outdoors, whitewater rafting, rock climbing, and all types of sports. I first got into mountain biking out of a desire to stay in shape, but my secret motivation is that I love the feeling of speeding almost out of control, racing down a hill toward a creek that I'll have to jump! I needed a bike that could hold up to all that punishment, so I bought the "Kona Coiler." It's bad to the bone! It has dual suspension and can travel on any terrain. It's sweet! That's my assessment now—but on the first day I rode it, I had a different opinion.

When I brought my new bike home, I was really pumped about my new toy. I hadn't ridden a bike in years, and the bikes I rode before were nothing like this one. When I do something, I go all out, so I got the coolest helmet, cut-finger gloves, breathable socks, and spiked shoes that hold your feet into the pedals. I mean, I got the whole deal!

As soon as I got all that equipment home, I put on my new gear and off I went. It took me a few seconds to figure out how to make the shoes fit into the pedal slots, but as I was pedaling down the street, I finally heard the click telling me that my shoes had locked into the fittings. I was now a pro—or so I thought. As I got to the end of the street, I got ready to make the turn toward the bike trail near our home. I slowed down as I approached the stop sign. At this strategic moment, I realized something terrible. I thought, "I'm coming to a busy intersection, and my feet are locked into these pedals. I have no idea how to get my feet out when I stop!"

As I slowed down, I frantically pulled on my feet, hoping that somehow the shoes would dislodge from the pedals so I could put one on the ground when I stopped. No matter how hard I pulled and pushed, my feet were stuck. It was as if they were bolted down. The bike slowly rolled to a stop with my feet still on the pedals. It was like a movie in slow motion. The last few feet took forever, but finally, I came to a complete stop—and the bike began to fall over. I hit the pavement with a huge thud!

Immediately, I felt tremendous pain. The physical pain was significant, but it didn't compare to the emotional pain I felt as I realized a car was at the intersection and the driver had witnessed me looking like a complete idiot! I can imagine him telling this story to his friends: "You should've seen this guy! As he came to the stop sign, he was jerking and pulling his legs, but he couldn't take his feet off the pedals. Then . . . Bam! He hit the pavement! It was hilarious! You should have seen it!"

But that's not all. The driver waited at the intersection to watch the rest of this act. It must have been more entertaining than any movie he'd seen lately. Imagine this. I continued to frantically pull and flail my legs to get my feet out of the pedals—while I was lying on the ground wrapped around my new bike! Finally, I twisted and contorted my body, and I got one foot out . . . and then the other. I was humiliated, but at least one person got a good laugh out of it.

Disgusted and demoralized, I walked the bike home. I wasn't ready to take it to the mountains . . . no matter how cool it looked and no matter how much gear I had bought. I needed to learn how to ride the bike so I could enjoy the trails in the mountains. (I soon learned that a certain twist of the foot enables you to get your feet out of the fittings on the pedals.) I needed instructions. I needed experience. I needed individual attention. I needed to be led!

As we return to our passage in Matthew 17, we read that Jesus "led them up on a high mountain by themselves." As I thought about this part of the passage, I realized why I had been so frustrated, so angry, so discouraged. I had been trying to live the Christian life the best I possibly could, but without individual attention from the Master. Was I busy serving Him? You bet. Was I intense and passionate? Actually, a little *too* intense and passionate. But my spiritual feet were stuck in the pedals of my life, and I was falling down over and over again. I was physically exhausted, but worse, I felt humiliated, confused, and ashamed. I thought, *Surely the abundant Christian life is better than this!*

What jumped off the page of the Bible in this passage was the word "led." I had tried to climb the mountain on my own. Effort, sweat, determination, and commitment weren't the problem. I had all of those, but Jesus hadn't led me. As I thought about this truth, my mind was on overload. That was when the Lord chided me, "Thomas, you can't go to the mountain on your own. You have to be led there—by Me."

To be led by Jesus means we see our selfish motives for what they are, reject them, and focus our hearts on the One who deserves every fiber of our affection and loyalty. We boycott our self-seeking agenda as we stand before His throne. We lay aside our ambitions, desires, wants, and personal quests, and we drive toward the heart of God.

In another conversation, Jesus told His followers that we must deny ourselves and take up our crosses and follow Him (Luke 9:23). He doesn't intend for us to deny our personalities or the strengths He has given us. Instead, He means for us to say no to the sinful, selfish part of ourselves. That's the part we deny in order to say yes to Christ and His purposes for us.

I needed leading.
I needed to recognize the mess I'd made
of trying to do it all on my own,
and I had to **surrender** to Him and allow
His **power** to **flow** out of my life.

As we drink from the life-giving grace of God, His love and strength flow from us. Jesus explained this phenomenon at a feast in Jerusalem. "Now on the last day, the great day of the feast, Jesus stood and cried out, saying, 'If anyone is thirsty, let him come to Me and drink. He who believes in Me, as the Scripture said, 'From his innermost being will flow rivers of living water.' But this He spoke of the Spirit" (John 7:37-39).

I had been thirsty, but I had gone to the wrong well to drink. I had gone to self-effort, success, and the desire for approval. I drank those things, and they satisfied me for a short time. But it was like drinking ocean water. Soon the effects of the bad water made me spiritually sick. My symptoms were discouragement, resentment, and confusion. In my foolishness, I thought that I just needed to drink more and more of the ocean water. But with every gulp, I got sicker and sicker. I needed—I desperately needed—to drink of Christ.

So instead of focusing on all I could do for God, I began looking at all He had done for me. That sounds simple, but my pride had clouded my vision of this clear and simple truth. Now, I wanted to take

Jesus' hand and be led by Him. I've heard drug addicts say that they had to come to a point of desperation, or "hitting bottom," to motivate them to change. That's what happened to me in a spiritual sense. I had tried to make the Christian life work, and the harder I tried, the more frustrated I became. Finally, I cried out to God for help. I had hit bottom, and God met me there with the simple word "led." Jesus led Peter, James, and John, and I longed for Him to lead me.

Was all of this new to me? Certainly not. I'd heard dozens of sermons about it, and I've preached a few of them myself. But preaching and living can be two different things. We've all heard one of the standard endings of formal prayers, "And now, Oh Lord, lead, guide, and direct us." That was now my true prayer. Now, I wanted more than anything to be led by God. I wanted to drink of Christ so His love and strength (and *only* His love and strength) would flow through me to others. I wanted Him to direct me in my marriage, in my relationships with my children and my best friends, with my neighbors, with people I speak to in my ministry, and with strangers everywhere I go. I wanted to take Jesus Christ out of any box I had put Him in. I wanted Him to have all of me, top to bottom, inside and out, all day every day.

For a horse to be led, it has to submit to the trainer or rider. For Christians to be led, we have to be led by Jesus. Ironically, submitting to God unlocks the door of passion in our hearts. As we surrender our wills to Him and desire to honor Him, we begin to see the wonder of His love more clearly. And as we see Him more clearly, we love Him more.

Richard Foster has written several books on the benefits of discipline in the Christian life. He warns against misunderstanding the concept of submission: "Most of us have been exposed to such a mutilated form of Biblical submission, that either we have embraced the deformity or we have rejected the discipline altogether."[10]

Do you want to go to the mountain? You'll have to be led there because you can't find it on your own. Is Jesus leading you? You'll have to be instructed by Him, so pay attention and learn the lessons He's teaching. Don't try it yourself or you'll fall over like I did on the bike I thought I could master on my own. You might end up walking home in embarrassment and shame.

There's a better way, the way of joy, peace, love, and fulfillment. But first, it's the way of submission and humility. Not everybody is willing to go that way. Some will insist on going their own way. They will experience some success, but sooner or later, they hit bottom. At that moment, they have a choice to make: Will they learn the lesson and reach out to Jesus to be led by Him, or will they grit their teeth and try it alone again?

Submitting to God is far easier when we realize how great is His sovereignty and love. Oswald Chambers was known for his piercing insights about humility and submission to God. He wrote, "Notion your mind with the idea that God is there. Nothing happens in any particular unless God's will is behind it, therefore you can rest in perfect confidence in Him."[11]

Do you want to be led by Jesus to the mountain?

Think about it...

1. Read John 7:37-39. What does spiritual thirst feel like? What can happen when we drink the wrong water to try to quench our thirst? What does Jesus promise to those who drink of Him?

2. Before you read this chapter, how would you have defined "submission"? How would you define it now?

3. Do you agree or disagree with the idea that we have to "hit bottom" before we'll trust God and submit to Him? Explain your answer.

4. Describe what it means to you to be led by Jesus.

"He was TRANSFIGURED before them..."

5

Sometimes our eyes

can deceive us.

When I was a college student in Oklahoma, I traveled one weekend to preach at a church in Kansas. A leader of the church called me a few weeks later. He said they really appreciated my message to the students, and they wanted to invite me to spend the summer at their church. At first I wasn't too excited about investing my valuable time in the lives of a few high school students who lived on the backside of nowhere. I had much bigger, much better, much more important plans . . . but God had His own plan for me, and His plan involved taking me to His classroom to learn a little humility.

When I arrived at the church at the beginning of the summer, I hadn't yet learned my lesson. I was sure I could transform this youth group into a bunch of radicals for Christ, but I would have to work really fast. One of the first items in my "fast track" plans to radicalize them was to take them witnessing on the streets of their little town. On Friday night about a week after I arrived, I gave them a little training, and we "cruised the strip" to share the gospel. It was great to get these students out of their comfort zone. They were terrified, so they had to depend on God to get them through. (Of course, this is not the only way—and not even the best way—to share the gospel, but God used it in a powerful way.)

During the summer, I took them out each Friday night. One night, after sharing the gospel on the streets, some students took me to the other side of town to share Christ with "an old man that lived in a tree." I remember thinking, *I can hardly believe a guy actually lives in a tree, but I'm sure stranger things have happened.* The students were excited to take me, and their excitement fueled my enthusiasm. Maybe, just maybe, God would use us to touch that man's life. Off we went. By now, it was late and very dark. The students pulled the car up and shined the headlights toward the tree. They pointed and said, "Do you see him, Thomas?"

At first I couldn't see anything, but they pointed to a particular spot, and sure enough, there he was! I could see him hunched over, sitting in the tree. As soon as I saw him, the students sped away, saying they were afraid of him. "Whoa! Wait a minute! Let's go back there!" I demanded they return to the tree so I could tell this poor soul about God's love.

After a few minutes of argument, they turned around drove back to the tree. I rolled down the window, leaned out, and yelled to him, "Jesus died on the cross to save us from our sins, and He rose from the grave. He's our Savior. Do you want Him to save you, too?"

In an instant, the student driving the car floored the accelerator and sped away. I was flabbergasted, then laughter erupted in the car. I was mad now. I demanded, "What's so funny?"

They didn't answer. They kept laughing so hard they were crying as they turned the car around again and drove back to that tree. They shined the lights of the car again where the "old man" was hunched over, and I saw what was so funny. What looked like a crouching old man was just a twisted branch . . . yep, a branch. The lights and shadows sure made it look like a man. I felt a little foolish, and more that a little humiliated. I had shared the gospel with a tree!

The second verse of Matthew 17 begins, "And He was transfigured before them. . . ." By this time, the disciples had been with Jesus for a couple of years. They had seen Him day and night, in cities and on the roads, in huge crowds and around lonely campfires. They thought they knew him really well, but they didn't. They were in for one of the biggest shocks of their lives! They needed to have their vision of Jesus expanded and sharpened, and Jesus knew just how to do it.

The disciples had seen Jesus perform countless miracles of healing, multiplying lunch, raising the dead, and casting out demons. They had seen Him perform only one other miracle involving Himself: walking on the water. But here, Peter, James, and John witnessed a spectacular event. As I reflected on this moment in the life of Jesus, it became a spectacular event in my life, too.

Jesus took those three people away from the normal busyness of life to a place where they could absorb the meaning of the moment. He had prepared them with months of teaching, miracles, and conversations. Now they were ready. On the mountain, Jesus changed His appearance so they could see Him in the awesome wonder of His nature.

IF JESUS' THREE DISCIPLES HAD ANY DOUBTS THAT HE WAS MORE THAN A MERE MORTAL, THOSE DOUBTS WOULD BE BLOWN AWAY BY THIS VISIBLE, INCREDIBLE REVELATION. HE DISPLAYED HIMSELF WITH THE RADIANCE OF HIS GLORY.

Most of us haven't thought much about the word "glory." It means something is awesome, majestic, and incomparable. The glory of Jesus Christ is the blend of His awful judgment and His tender mercy. We can't put Him in a box! No matter how much we learn about Him, He's far grander than we can imagine. His creative power and sovereign rule over the universe are beyond anything we can possibly conceive; His love is more passionate than anything we can imagine; and His wisdom is more penetrating than any human understanding. He is the king, not of the mightiest nation on earth, but of the entire universe! And since He created the universe, He is even greater.

In an attempt to describe the complexity and wonder of Christ's power and character, the great Puritan pastor Jonathan Edwards said that Jesus had "an admirable conjunction of diverse excellencies." Amen to that!

At the transfiguration, Jesus removed the blinders that had hidden Him from the disciples. Jesus transcended who they thought He was to reveal who He really is: the glory of the Father! They needed to know that He wasn't just some ordinary person. No. He proved to them that He was the awesome "I Am," Jehovah, the covenant-keeping God of Moses. The Jews revered the name Jehovah so much that they never spoke it. Here, Jesus identifies Himself with the Father, and He shares the glory of the Father. Jesus was a great teacher, the promised Messiah, the Son of God, our Lord and Savior. But beyond that, He is one with the Father and shares His glory. The writer to the Hebrews tells us,

"And [Jesus] is the radiance of [God's] glory and the exact representation of His nature" (Hebrews 1:3).

Because actions are visible, we often evaluate people based on what they do, where they go, and what they accomplish. That's natural and normal. But people are more than the sum total of their actions. Their identity is found in their family origin, their character, and their values. In the same way, it's easy for us to focus our attention on the activities of Jesus. Those actions are incredible, but they only give us part of the picture. We also need to understand His relationship to the Father and the Spirit. His identity unfolds as we examine His character and His values. As our grasp of Him grows, our worship becomes more passionate and joyful.

I can imagine the look on the faces of Peter, James, and John! But remember, they didn't tell Jesus they wanted to see His glory. They had done nothing to initiate the event. They had simply made themselves available, and Jesus selected them for this moment.

In our lives, too, God must show us Himself. Augustine was one of the most influential believers in all of Christian history. His grasp of God's grace came from his experience of Christ's forgiveness for his sinfulness. In reflecting on our need to see Jesus more clearly as the great "I Am," Augustine built his insights on the back of another lion of the faith, Ambrose. Augustine wrote:

"As Ambrose says, 'No man has the power in himself to envision God as He truly is. Yet, there are situations that cause God to reveal something of Himself to men—and to some men in partic-ular, because of the circumstances in which they find themselves. In those cases, a man "merits" a clearer vision of God because of the occasion. Then God reveals Himself and it is purely an act of grace.' And yet there is another matter here. Sometimes we do not merit seeing God in a difficult occasion, because we have not cultivated grace in our inner man. We have not sought God in order to grow in grace. That is to say, we do not merit the honor of being set by God in difficult circumstances—situations in which He wants to be made known, because we have not grown in our ability to see Him in our inner man."[12]

Jesus picks whomever He wants to pick, and we choose to be avail-able to go with Him to the mountain. We long for His presence, and we wait to experience the wonder of Him on the journey!

Do you want to go to the mountain? It will mean being in the presence of Jesus and experiencing the glory of God!

Think about it . . .

1. Can you think of an instance when you were fooled about some-thing you thought you saw? Describe how you felt when you realized you were wrong.

_____

2. How do you think you would have responded if you had been Peter, James, or John at the moment when Jesus was transfigured before them?

3. Have you known Jesus for a while, as His disciples had? How would grasping God's glory affect your relationship with God, your desire to please Him, and your goals and ambitions?

4. If you are completely honest with yourself, do you really want to sense the awesome glory of Christ? Why or why not?

"and **HIS FACE** shone like the sun . . ."

6

Sacred soil.

I stepped off of the plane in Uganda, Africa, to speak to pastors and their congregations. At first I thought I was there only to minister to them. Soon, though, I realized I was the one who would be touched by God. The lessons I learned in that war-torn, poverty-stricken land changed my life. I learned about values. The incredible wealth of America is in its possessions, but the wealth possessed by the Christians of Uganda is their realization that they possess almost nothing, and they value their few possessions as meaningless. What matters to them is Jesus Christ. I had no idea how much all the tangible, physical, visible wealth in America had stolen my "pure and simple devotion to Christ." That was the lesson I would learn during those days in Africa.

Erin and I were honored to be there and deeply humbled by everything we saw. We were touched by the sheer delight the Ugandan people expressed. They were genuinely thrilled with God and what He was doing in their lives.

I was there to teach over 800 pastors and preach to the crowds at nightly meetings in two different cities. Erin was scheduled to speak to women in many different villages and cites. At one of the first places where she spoke, the ladies greeted her waving palm branches. In another place, they had saved their money (what little they had) and bought her some very special and expensive tea. We found out later that they had spent a month's wages on the tea and other gifts to honor her. We were continually amazed at the generosity, love, care, and sincerity of the people. We were there to touch them, but God used them to touch us.

Two remarkable events allowed me to see below the surface of poverty and want. Those situations enabled me to see people whose lives were consumed with the things of God. The two events spoke deeply to my heart about how true followers of Christ walk with Him in love and integrity. These people were treading on sacred soil.

The first event occurred during the one of the nightly meetings. Earlier in the day, I had overheard a man proclaiming his Muslim faith and was reminded of how Islam heavily influenced that city. That evening I was on stage speaking about the cross of Christ. I was preaching with passion, and I sensed the anointing of God. After I had finished speaking that night, I asked if anyone would like to follow Jesus Christ. If they were hearing the call of God to repentance and faith in Jesus Christ, I invited them to walk forward and stand in front of the stage. But no one did that. Apparently they sensed God moving in a far more powerful way. Instead of walking forward, they ran forward and jumped up on the stage! Men and women, young and old—they came with brokenness and sincerity. I was touched by their response to God's grace. Soon the stage was packed with repentant people, but more of them kept running forward. There was no stopping them now! They were running to their God!

The second pivotal event happened at one of the pastors' conferences. For several days, we had been sharing, teaching, preaching, and pouring our lives into the attendees. The conference was scheduled to end the next day at noon. After the last nightly session of the conference, the wife of one of the leading pastors was eating dinner at our hotel with our team. It was getting very late. We noticed she was extremely tired, and she needed a ride back to the church. She appeared to be concerned about the lateness of the hour.

When I asked, she told me that she had a lot to do when she got back. It was past 11 p.m., and I asked her what she could still have to do. She said, "I need to cook." I must have had a curious expression on my face, so she continued, "I need to cook breakfast for the pastors you will speak to tomorrow morning. Many of them have been staying at the church." (Their church was a building with a dirt floor, a wooden frame, and cardboard from boxes for siding).

I asked her how many pastors were staying there. She said, "About two hundred or so." Wow! Two hundred pastors had been sleeping on the ground or on the benches each night, and this precious pastor's wife was cooking for them each day. Why? So they could be trained in the Word of God and become more effective in communicating the love and power of Christ.

I was dumbfounded. These men had been staying there each night, and she had been working hard to feed them—simply because she wanted to glorify God. The next morning we gave away two hundred bicycles to pastors so they could have transportation to take the Word of God out to places where the gospel had never been preached. As those dear men of God received their bikes, we watched them shout and cry with joy.

Matthew tells us that when the appearance of Jesus was changed, "His face shone like the sun, and His garments became as white as light." This, I'm quite sure, was one of those times when words simply can't express the grandeur of the moment. Images of light are used often in the Bible to depict the glory of God. In John's revelation, he describes a vision of the risen Christ that includes dazzling light and whiteness. His account includes the statement: "In His right hand He held seven stars; and out of His mouth came a sharp two-edged sword; and His face was like the sun shining in its strength" (Revelation 1:16).

One moment there were three men standing on a mountain with Jesus. Suddenly, His face, His clothes, and everything about Him radically changed. The next moment the three disciples were looking at the radiance of the glory of God! As mortal men, they got a glimpse of the risen, immortal, glorified Savior who will return one day looking just as He did that day!

To really know Jesus Christ, we have to look beyond the limitations He placed on Himself when He walked on earth. We have to see Him as John saw Him in his revelation, as Isaiah saw Him in his vision, and as the three disciples saw Him on the mountain that day. While He was on earth, Jesus humbled Himself to die for us, but He's not in human form any longer! He is risen, glorified, and awesome. When John saw the vision of Christ in His glory, he was overcome. John "fell at His feet as a dead man" (Revelation 1:17). John, probably the person who was Jesus' closest friend on earth, fainted when He saw Jesus as He really is! What does that say to you and me?

We have to look beyond the garments to see Christ's glory.

We need to get past the superficial to get to the supernatural. This principle has several implications. We need to get beyond any shallow perception of Christ. Yes, Jesus calls us His friends, but He is an awesome, majestic, overwhelmingly powerful friend. Yes, He was tender, meek, and mild, but He is the incomparable creator and ruler of the universe. Yes, He died on the cross to forgive our sins, but He's coming back to claim His own and render judgment on those who reject Him.

As I thought about the meaning of the Matthew 17:1-8 passage, I realized that I was far too preoccupied with the superficial "garments" of religious activities. I did a lot of good things simply because they were expected of me. Sooner or later, those activities became routine, and I became focused on the activities instead of on God. As my focus drifted, I missed the main point: Jesus Himself. I had gradually started using Jesus to accomplish my own goals. My attitude was, "Jesus, help me be more successful and happy." But Jesus didn't come to earth, suffer, and die to make me successful and happy. He came to rescue me from my selfishness, set me free, and transform my desires so that I want to glorify Him more than anything in the world!

Do you need to look beyond the garments to see Jesus' glory? If you and I are serious about knowing God, from time to time we may realize that our focus has drifted to the externals. During those moments, we need to repent, to change course, and come back to the light of Jesus' glorious face. When we do, we'll realize how much we've missed in those weeks, months, or (God forbid) years that our gaze has been fixed on superficial things instead of the awesome, wonderful, tender, powerful face of Christ.

Matthew tells us that Jesus wasn't alone at the moment of His transfiguration: "And behold, Moses and Elijah appeared to them, talking with Him" (Matthew 17:3). Moses probably felt right at home because he had visited God on a different mountain and experienced His glory.

After Moses met with God on Mt. Sinai, the people saw "that the skin of Moses' face shone. So Moses would replace the veil over his face until he went in to speak with [God]" (Exodus 34:35). Like Moses, we are changed when we see God's glory. In fact, people can tell a big difference in us!

To be honest with you, this insight was very painful for me. I realized that I look far too much at Jesus' human form than His eternal glory, and my faith has suffered because of it. But I long for more. I long to be overwhelmed by the intensity of the vision of Christ's magnificence! I want to be so blown away by an accurate perception of Christ that, like John, I fear I'll faint!

Augustine understood the importance of seeing Christ as the glorified, majestic, awesome God of the universe. He wrote, "And since all those who think of God think of something living, only they can think of Him without absurdity who think of Him as life itself."[13]

If you and I want to go to the mountain, we have to look past the human garments to see Him as He really is. Then and only then, as Augustine said, we can think of Him as life itself.

The believers in Uganda taught me a lot about Christ. In their poverty, they believed in His riches, kindness, and greatness. They didn't value physical possessions. Instead, they looked beyond the seen to the unseen. They beheld the glory of God! Their perception of Christ is a sweet picture that has helped cut away the residue of superficial things in my life. I have a long way to go . . . but I'm going . . . to the mountain!

Do you still want to go to the mountain so you can see Christ's magnificence?

Think about it . . .

1. Read Revelation 1:12-18. What are some reasons it's important to have a clearer picture of the risen, glorified Christ?

2. In what ways has your life been focused on the superficial, the tangible, the seen? How has that focus affected your faith?

3. What would it mean to you to grasp far more of the magnificence of the glory of Christ? How would it affect your purpose in life, your attitude, and your relationships?

"Lord, IT IS GOOD for us to be here."

7

I'm in the middle of nowhere.

I'm alone in a small ranch house in the vast expanse of the middle of Texas. I needed to carve out some time to think, pray, and write this book. When God first showed me these truths from Matthew 17, it was just for me. I was a dry, thirsty soul, and I desperately needed God to give me a tall, cool drink of His Spirit. The insights God gave me changed my life, and of course, I couldn't help but share those insights with others. The transfiguration of Jesus was no longer just a sermon to be preached or one of the stories of the Bible. It became a journey to the ultimate reality: Christ Himself.

It was difficult to find time to be alone for the exclusive purpose of writing. I have a beautiful wife and three incredible children. Erin knew God had put this message on my heart, and she wanted me to be able to put it down on paper, but I just couldn't do that at home. I have no doubt that God gave me this message. I wasn't a professor looking for a great lesson to teach my students in class. I was a frustrated, desperate man searching for a handle on life. God reached into my pain and spoke to my heart.

I needed this sabbatical to write. Out here on the plains of Texas, I look at the rolling terrain and hear the noise of insects and birds. I'm a lot like Peter, who said at a time of wonder, "It is good for me to be here."

Don't you love Peter? At one of the most powerful and poignant moments recorded in history, God Himself changed His appearance to communicate His glory to three handpicked men. Impetuous Peter just couldn't stand there and say nothing, so he said something stupid! "Hey, ain't it great to be here?" We can laugh at Peter's impulsive comment, but I think he had a valuable insight at that moment.

The sight of the change in Jesus' appearance genuinely blew Peter away. In fact, he was thrilled that Jesus had selected him to see this, and his statement was one of appreciation. What do you think it meant for Peter to be on that mountain that day? I think it had everything to do with his feeling accepted, believed in, and trusted. Jesus didn't take everybody to the mountain—just three of His men. Peter realized that Jesus had given him one of the greatest honors ever bestowed on anyone, and he was thankful.

Peter's statement had two important implications: one for that moment, and one for later. The first implication is that this honor brought a new, deeper intimacy to Peter's relationship with Jesus. When a close friend tells you a secret, you treasure not just the secret itself, but the trust shown in you by your friend. In the same way, this event was a type of secret between Jesus and the three men. As we'll see later, when they walked down the mountain, Jesus instructed them not to tell anybody about the monumental event until after the resurrection. He would later appear to the disciples, the women, and a group of 500 who saw Him at one time. In those post-resurrection appearances He looked just like He appeared to Peter, James, and John on the mountain. They could then say, "We've seen Him look like that before!"

Trust builds intimacy, and secrets kept build trust. That's why it was "good" for Peter to be there with Jesus. Jesus had trusted three of His followers so much that He allowed them to see something no one else had seen. Peter sensed that, and it drew him to Jesus even more closely.

I need to be "with Jesus" in such a close, personal way, too. I need more than a fun Bible study or a meaningful church service. Those are terrific, but I need more. I need to enter the secret place where I can see Jesus far more clearly and be overwhelmed by His glory.

What are you thinking right now? Do you long for this kind of intimacy with Christ? I didn't ask if you have prayed or read your Bible or been to church—all of which can be encouraging. But there's more.

Stop and ask God for a fresh, vivid sense of His presence. Think about what it means to treasure His love and be amazed by His awesome power. The presence of God can be comforting, but it can also overwhelm us.

Years ago, Brother Lawrence wrote and spoke about "practicing the presence of God." He commented, "I cannot imagine how religious persons can live satisfied without the practice of the presence of God."[14]

Moses and Elijah appear on the scene with Jesus, and their presence validates the authenticity of the encounter. They represent the Law (Moses) and the prophets (Elijah). If the transcendent glow of Jesus' face and garments didn't get the message across, the presence of Moses and Elijah communicated to Peter (and to us all) that Jesus is God in all of His glory. The law and the prophets foretold the coming Messiah, God in the flesh. Now, on that mountain, Peter, James, and John saw even more clearly that this Jesus they had been following was indeed the Christ, the Son of the Living God.

The journey of walking with God sometimes goes through valleys, sometimes climbs the sides of mountains, and sometimes takes us to the mountain peaks. The image we gain of Christ's glory on the top of the mountain can sustain us in times of difficulty, confusion, and the routines of normal life. When Peter, James, and John came down from the mountain, I'm sure they never forgot the experience. The sight of Jesus glowing in all of His glory was etched on their minds and hearts for the rest of their lives. It can be etched on ours, too.

The second implication of Peter's statement speaks to his betrayal of Jesus on the night He was arrested. Because Jesus trusted Peter by taking him up the mountain to witness His glory, Peter didn't have to wonder if Jesus' promise to forgive him was valid. Jesus, Peter became convinced, could do anything! He could even forgive someone who denied Him three times in His hour of need. That night, ashamed and humiliated, Peter went out and wept bitterly.

After Christ was raised from the dead, He found Peter and asked him three times, "Peter, do you love me?" The symmetry is beautiful, isn't it? Three denials, then three questions, and three affirmations of loyalty. I can imagine that the image of Jesus on that mountain made Peter's denials even more bitter, but that memory also reminded Peter that Jesus, the Holy God, had the power to forgive him.

In a beautiful psalm of repentance, the psalmist showed the connection between forgiveness and the awesome power of God. He wrote:

"If You, Lord, should mark iniquities,
    O Lord, who could stand?
But there is forgiveness with You,
    That You may be feared" (Psalm 130:3-4).

There is a "sixth sense" in the lives of those going to the mountain. When you experience the presence of Jesus, your life will be radically transformed.

THEN—AND ONLY THEN— YOU WILL BE ENTRANCED WITH HIS GLORY. YOU WILL BE ENTHRALLED WITH HIS CHARACTER. YOU WILL WANT TO BE ENTRENCHED IN HIS WORD. AND THEN YOU WILL BE ENGULFED IN HIS POWER.

Like Peter, you too will say: It is good for me to be here!

I'm still in the middle of nowhere on the plains of Texas, but I'm in the presence of Almighty God. As I sit here, my heart's cry is: "Jesus, I want to see You, know You, and trust You for who You really are. I want to be so blown away by Your presence that I'll say, Lord, it's good to be here! Please continue to take me to the mountain!"

Do you want to go to the mountain to experience intimacy with God?

Think about it . . .

1. Describe some ways it was "good" for Peter to witness the transfiguration of Jesus. What did it do to him, for him, and in him?

2. What does it mean for you to have intimacy with someone so awesome?

3. Does it help to remember the transcendent greatness of God when we sin and need to be forgiven? Explain your answer.

"while he was STILL SPEAKING . . ." (Part 1)

8

Why am I on

the side of the road?

That was the question one night while I was a college student in Oklahoma. I was driving back to school after a weekend at home, and I was having a great time cruising along the interstate listening to music. It was dusk, and in Oklahoma the orange glow of the sky is pretty spectacular. Some clouds began to form, then it started to sprinkle tiny drops of rain. That was fine with me because it had been

105

a hot day, and I was glad to cool off. I turned on the windshield wipers and kept driving.

I was about thirty minutes away from the university when I noticed that my car seemed to be losing power. Even though I was pressing harder on the accelerator, the car continued to slow down. A few minutes later I noticed the lights on the dashboard, and even my headlights, were getting dim. Then my radio quit working. My windshield wipers began to crawl slowly across the windshield, and eventually they came to a halt. Finally, the car died. I had no clue what was wrong.

I'm not a "car guy," but I sure didn't want to look helpless. Acting like a competent, strong, resourceful man, I popped the hood so I could pretend like I knew what I was doing. (That's what you are supposed to do if you want to appear to be a man who's completely in control. It's called "ego." On a number of occasions, God has shown me how big a problem this ego thing is for me. This was going to be one of those times!) I couldn't see anything wrong with the engine. I checked the connections to the battery. I checked the belts, the hoses, and everything else. Then I got back in the car and turned the key. I was hoping that somehow . . . but nothing. Not even a sound.

I walked through a field to a nearby house and called a friend at school. He came in his truck and towed my car back to the dorm. The next day, we determined that I needed a new battery. The one in the car wasn't old, but it simply didn't have any juice. When we tried to use jumper cables to start the car, it wouldn't even turn over. Dead as a doornail.

We drove into town where I bought a new battery. We put it in, and the car started immediately. Man, I love that sound!

The next day, I was back on the interstate headed out of town. I was listening to the radio. The windshield wipers were doing their thing because I was in another rainstorm. I was cruising down the road, and "it was déjà vu all over again"! The car started losing power. The windshield wipers slowed and then stopped. I was going 60, then 40, 30, 20, 10. . . and then stopped. I thought, *What's the deal? It can't be the battery.* But there I was, once more stuck on the side of the road.

Yet again, my friend came to my rescue. When he got there, we examined the car very carefully. We noticed that the indicator light on the dash showed that the battery was down. We tried to recharge it, but it wouldn't keep the charge. For the second day in a row, we took it back and got another battery. I was certain that the first battery had died of natural causes and the second one was defective. I'd just been unlucky. The third battery, I was sure, would do the trick.

Wrong!

I drove away from the shop with my brand new battery, but soon I was stuck on the side of the road again! Again, nothing looked wrong, but I needed help.

I took the car to a mechanic who quickly identified the problem. He told me the alternator was defective. I'd blown a lot of money on my first two repair attempts, so I needed to save a dollar this time. I bought an alternator and installed it in the parking lot of my dorm. Problem solved (at last).

This story illustrates three kinds of people:

- Some of us are clueless. Our lives are stuck, and we don't know what the problem is.
- Many of us focus on a superficial problem and miss the real, underlying one.
- A few of us have insight into the real issues in life. Like a master mechanic, we can diagnose the real problem so we can find the right solution.

I learned an important principle from this situation:

> It doesn't matter how good things look on the outside. If you're stuck on the side of the road, you've got a problem that needs to be addressed. And worse, you might not even know it!

Reviewing our examination of Jesus on the mountain with His disciples, His appearance had radically changed. It was awesome! And then two other guys suddenly appeared—Moses and Elijah. Man, this was amazing!

Peter chose that moment to announce his plan for a commemoration of the event. He volunteered to build three shelters. But in the middle of his little speech, notice what happened. Matthew tells us,

"While he was still speaking, a bright cloud overshadowed them." Did you see it? Peter was interrupted.

This was no ordinary interruption. It wasn't a friend who wanted a piece of your pizza or a stranger asking for directions. It wasn't a child who wanted to be held or a spouse who needed some attention. It was God Almighty breaking into Peter's discourse.

As I thought about this particular moment in the drama, it hit me like a ton of bricks: I often spend time mumbling my perceptions about life to Jesus, when in reality, He wants me to be quiet and listen to Him! I'm like Peter; I need for God to interrupt me. And that's exactly what this passage does for me—it interrupts my self-centered, ego-driven purposes and says, "Hey, Thomas, it might be wise for you to, well, shut up and listen for a change." When I think I know what God wants, when I think I have all the answers, when I think I have the best plans for other people . . . I need to be interrupted.

How about you? Are there times when you need to be interrupted, to be put in your place and be reminded to listen? (If your answer is, "Yes, but not as often as you, Thomas," I think I'd agree with you!)

How does God interrupt us? He doesn't usually come to us in a cloud and a thundering voice, so how does He get our attention? I believe God uses all kinds of things to interrupt us. He uses difficulties, great worship music, the laughter of a child, the touch of a friend, the power of His Word, and countless other means. The problem is not that God doesn't try to interrupt us. The problem is our interpretation of the interruption.

If I think the interruption is an obstacle to fulfilling my goals, I'll resent it instead of valuing it. Far too often, that's how I see difficulties: simply as obstacles to be overcome instead of messages from God to stop, look, and listen to Him. And I take the positive interruptions for granted. A word of kindness, fun with friends, a beautiful sunset, and a thousand other gifts from God are easily passed over and unappreciated. The more I think about it, I believe God wants to interrupt me a hundred times a day to remind me of His love, forgiveness, creativity, and power.

Can you identify some divine interruptions you've experienced (or missed) today? They are important ingredients of a life of intimacy on the mountain.

Don't get left on the side of the road. Don't let your battery run down, and if it does, make sure you check the deeper issues of your life: your purpose, your trust in God's sovereignty, and your faith in His forgiveness. Pay attention. Everything in your life might look fine on the surface, but there might be a hidden problem.

God will interrupt whenever He pleases. Take the time to stop, look, and listen to Him so that you can enjoy the long ride. When you find yourself on the side of the road, be wise and look for the real issues. See every difficulty as a reminder of your dependence on God, and every blessing as a gift from God. Both are His interruptions.

Are you willing to be interrupted on your way to the mountain?

Think about it . . .

1. Why do you think God interrupted Peter?

2. How do you think Peter responded to this awesome interruption of the cloud and the voice of God?

3. What are some reasons why God might want to interrupt us?

---

4. See if you can identify some recent interruptions you've experienced. How will you recognize them better from now on? How will you respond?

"while he was STILL SPEAKING . . ." (Part 2)

9

Why did God

interrupt Peter when He did?

In the last chapter, we explored the implications of divine interruptions in our lives, but we never got around to revealing what Peter was doing at the time. Did you notice?

Peter was talking to Jesus. That's a good thing to do, isn't it? So far, so good. However, "good things" aren't necessarily "God things." In fact, we can fill our lives with so many good things that they crowd out the God things. At this monumental moment on the mountain, God wanted Peter to watch, listen, and absorb the incredible power and beauty of intimacy with the transfigured Jesus. That was the "God thing"! But Peter was preoccupied with his own agenda of planning his response to the sight and telling Jesus his plans. Talking to Jesus . . . yes, Peter was praying.

Prayer is one of the foundations of the Christian life, and in fact, Paul told the believers in Thessalonica to "pray without ceasing" (1 Thess. 5:17). So what's the problem? Why did God interrupt Peter?

When I speak on this topic in churches and ask this question, a lot of congregations get quiet . . . really quiet. The insights God gave me about this point in the passage have been penetrating and liberating. It was a jolt of joy. But I needed this jolt to sink deep into my heart and become a lifestyle for me.

Talking to Jesus is a good thing, and that's what Peter was doing. The reason for God's interruption was that Peter was involved in a good thing, but not a God thing! Prayer is good, but it wasn't what God wanted Peter to do at that moment.

As I reflected on this concept, I quickly saw that my life was littered with good things that might, and sometimes did, interfere with the best things God wanted for me. I enjoy sports, great movies, hanging out with friends, playing with the children, spending time with Erin, doing a good job traveling and speaking, helping people in need, and dozens of other things. None of these are wrong, but they can gradually creep into the center of my life, crowd Jesus out, and take His place. That's when good things become wrong things.

Everything in our lives can be a "God thing" if we use it to honor Christ. Yes, everything. Even the most mundane activities honor God if we do them thankfully and with excellence. Paul wrote, "Whether, then, you eat or drink or whatever you do, do all to the glory of God" (1 Cor. 10:31). No task is too menial. Even the slaves of Paul's day could honor God as they did their work. He told them, "Slaves, in all things obey those who are your masters on earth, not with external service, as those who merely please men, but with sincerity of heart, fearing the Lord. Whatever you do, do your work heartily, as for the Lord rather than for men; knowing that from the Lord you will receive the reward of the inheritance. It is the Lord Christ whom you serve" (Col. 3:22-24).

If slaves can honor God in their attitudes and behavior, surely you and I can, too. The issue is not that we lack opportunities. The issue is our hearts: Do we want to honor God, or do we want to please ourselves?

In our culture, we do a lot of things to fit in, to look good, to be accepted by people we value. Many of us, in fact, tailor our decisions for precisely that purpose. The way we talk, the things we buy, the way we look, and the possessions we own are designed to win acceptance. When we value others' opinions so highly, though, we crowd God out of the center of our hearts. And anything we put before Christ becomes an idol. Paul told the Galatians, "For am I now seeking the favor of men, or of God? Or am I striving to please men? If I were still trying to please men, I would not be a bond-servant of Christ" (Gal. 1:10).

We are either bond-servants of God, or we are bond-servants of the people we please. We can't have it both ways. Even good things become hindrances to our relationship with God when they take the place of God in our hearts.

One of the ways I can tell if something is a good thing or a God thing is very simple: Did I pray about it? Did I even take the time to reflect on this purchase or that conversation, accepting this job or deciding to watch that movie? If I haven't prayed, then I may not have brought God into the decision-making process at all. No, the possession or activity may not be evil, wrong, or destructive, but if I'm not even aware of how I can use it to honor God, I'll probably miss the opportunity.

In America, we are incredibly wealthy. We have almost anything we want, but sadly, many of us gripe and complain because we don't have as much as this person or that person. Comparison usually produces the bitter fruit of discontent, and that's not a fruit we should be eating! People in our culture are consumed with a passion to experience the good life, but that passion takes us in the wrong direction, away from God, truth, peace, and the beautiful things He wants us to enjoy.

In the church today, many of us are preoccupied with "good things." We want God to make us feel good, and we want to be entertained by the services. If one church doesn't make us feel just right, we go somewhere else. God wants us to grow beyond the infant stage of thinking that all of life is about us. As we mature, we learn that God has a purpose for us that is far bigger, far grander, far more meaningful than anything we can imagine. As we get involved in helping and serving, we develop a stronger relationship with God because we have to depend on Him for wisdom and direction. Our relationships with others grow deeper, and our sense of fulfillment skyrockets.

Certainly, some of us are wounded and broken and need to focus on our hurts for a while to find healing. But for the rest of us, the goal of life is not entertainment; it's to follow Christ wherever He takes us. That journey is often fun and exciting, but sooner or later He takes us through the school of higher learning. When difficulties force us to trust Him more than ever, we're not out of God's will. We're right in the middle of it. A preoccupation with good things, however, is an obstacle to the rich, rewarding life God wants for us.

Do you want to go to the mountain? On the journey or at the top, you'll need to get rid of the "good things" and get into the "God things." For too many of us, the American dream is filling our lives with fun and challenging activities. Again, there's nothing inherently wrong with clubs, hobbies, sports, and any of dozens of other possibilities, but we have to jealously guard our hearts to make sure those good things don't crowd out our first priority of intimacy with God.

Many of us need to stop doing some of the good things we're doing right now so we can focus more of our time, energy, and passion on Christ. I know men who have chosen to go fishing less often, women who resign from a club or organization that was absorbing their time, and students who dropped out of cheerleading or a sport because they realized these activities stole their hearts away from Jesus.

It takes courage to tell someone, "I'd really like to join you in that, but it's not a priority for me right now." But there will come a day when we'll give an explanation to someone far more important. We certainly want Him to say we made the right choices.

And let me be perfectly honest here. For some of us, serving in the church has become a good thing that absorbs our time and energies. We began serving because we wanted to honor God and show our appreciation for His grace in our lives, but somewhere along the way, joyful service became drudgery. We've become tired and resentful, and our service is a hindrance to intimacy with God.

Before you make decisions—for yourself, your spouse, and your children—to be involved in clubs, jobs, and any other activity, and before you make a major purchase, ask God if it's the best thing. And wait for His answer. Don't let another week, month, or year go by when you wonder, "Is this all there is?" Don't settle for less than the excitement of following God's path. Intimacy with God is our first and highest priority. From that deep well of love and energy comes a river of wisdom to guard our hearts as we pursue joyful, targeted activity that pleases Him.

Do you really want to go to mountain where you can throw away a lot of good things and focus instead on the God things?

Think about it . . .

1. Describe the process of how good things can become obstacles in our journey to know and serve God wholeheartedly.

2. How does comparison focus our attention on good things and leave us longing for more of them instead of longing for Christ?

3. What are some good things in your life that threaten your journey? What are you going to do about them?

_____

"A BRIGHT CLOUD
overshadowed them . . ."

10

I hated my dad.

I grew up in a dysfunctional home. My parents divorced when I was about 12, and our family experienced a bitter custody battle. I don't blame my mom at all for wanting a divorce because my dad was incredibly difficult to live with. Often he ignored my sister and me. The pain this caused was intense and dreadful. It caused me to have a deep disdain for him. Yet I went to live with my dad because after the divorce, he was a nicer person. And I know now that my dad was miserable himself. He was unhappy and without a relationship with Christ.

My dad didn't claim to be a Christian when I was a boy. Neither did I, but after the first semester of my freshman year of college, Christ changed my life! As I experienced the love and forgiveness of God, I gradually began to genuinely love my dad. That's what happens when you are born again. You go from darkness to light, hell to heaven, and hate to love. So with this newly found love for God and my dad, I asked God for ways to show my dad that Jesus is the Savoir he needed.

One night I was talking with my college roommate, Joel. (He was the best man in my wedding, and still is my best friend.) We were on the church steps praying when Joel looked at me and said, "Thomas, if you could ask God for anything in the world and He'd give to you, what would you ask for?"

That was easy. I told Joel that I wanted God to work in my dad's heart to lead him to Christ. I wanted my dad to know the same joy and peace I had found in my relationship with Christ. Joel immediately said, "Let's pray for him." The two of us spent an intense time bringing my father to the throne of God. We prayed that God would soften his heart, awaken him to the truth of the gospel, and give him faith to respond to God's amazing grace.

At the time, my father's heart was like concrete. He had no interest in God, the gospel, church, the three wise men, or anything else remotely connected to faith. When Joel and I prayed that night, my dad was 63 years old. I knew God could do anything, but in the back of my mind, I understood that it was statistically improbable. Very few people become followers of Christ after the age of 25, much less at 63!

Many months later, I was a student in seminary. I was going to preach at a church the next week, so I had to make arrangements with my professors. Since I was gone so much, they required me to attend every class when I was in town. As I prayed about my upcoming trip, the Holy Spirit impressed on me that I needed to get in my car and drive back to see my dad that day. I resisted because it didn't make sense. I was leaving for a trip the next day, and my profs required my attendance in class.

Then I remembered the night Joel and I had prayed together for my dad. Joel had shared with me some encouragement about God saving my dad and changing his life, so I drove from seminary in Texas to the ranch where my dad lives and spent the day with him. He had just gone through his third divorce, and he seemed very distant. He had heard the gospel a number of times in his life, and had even come to hear me speak on a few occasions. In addition, some of his neighbors and friends had invited him to church and had been witnessing to him about the grace of God.

As the day progressed, I looked for opportunities to share the gospel with him again, but it was difficult to find an opening. I wondered why God had wanted me to drive up to see him, but I knew He had called me to go. Late in the afternoon, it was time for me to leave. I had to drive back to catch my plane the following day. I walked out to the car and my dad followed me, which certainly wasn't normal. He never walked me out and usually didn't even say goodbye.

I put my bag down by the car, and God prompted me to walk over and give my dad a hug. As I hugged him, the Holy Spirit prompted me to whisper in his ear, "I love you, dad." I had committed two cardinal sins in my family: you definitely didn't hug dad or say you loved each other!

At that moment, my dad began to cry. I hadn't seen tears in his eyes since I was a little boy. He gently pushed me away and briskly walked back into the house. I got in the car and cried all the way back to Fort Worth. I kept thinking, *What was all of that about? God, why didn't you save my dad today? Why didn't I get to see him become a believer?*

I arrived back at the seminary and went to sleep. The next morning I was making coffee in the kitchen, and I noticed that someone had left a message on the answering machine. I pushed the button and listened to the message. It was my dad. He had called in the early hours of the morning. I heard him say, "Son, I wanted you to be the first to know that Jesus Christ is my Savior, and His Holy Spirit lives in my heart."

Wow! My dad was saved. My dad was born again. It happened!

In the years since that day, my father has been on mission trips, passed out Bibles in the Ukraine, helped start a homeless shelter, and reads the Bible as if it were his last day on earth. His story is one of the greatest Christian testimonies of God's power I've ever heard. He is totally changed—and so is our relationship.

In Matthew's account of Christ's life, he tells of the awesome change in Jesus' appearance. As Peter spoke, God interrupted with a visible sign of His presence. Matthew tells us, "A bright cloud over-shadowed them."

HE OVERSHADOWED THEM!

When we go to the mountain, something very strange happens: God overshadows us. He meets us there, amazes us with His glory, and we become thrilled to offer Him the praise He deserves. We are glad to acknowledge His power, His love, and His glory. That's the way John the Baptist felt about Jesus when he told people, "He must increase, but I must decrease" (John 3:30).

To be overshadowed is at once comforting and challenging. We recognize that we aren't the center of the universe any longer (that's the challenging part!), and we realize that God's rightful place is high up on His throne. There, we worship Him, and He nourishes us. Charles Spurgeon wrote about the joy of being overshadowed by God: "Under His shadow we are to feel that we are at home. After that, He will make Himself at home to us by becoming food for our souls and by giving spiritual refreshment to us while we rest."[15]

Everyone on the mountain that day was overshadowed: Peter, James, John, Moses, and Elijah. The only one left in full view was Jesus. God wants all of us to live an overshadowed life. Then, the only one we care to see is Jesus, and the only thing people see in us is Jesus. If we grasp the greatness of God, we'll desire the overshadowed life that God offers. But do we really want that? I believe God delights in our prayers for Him to overshadow us. It's a prayer of joyful surrender. We want Him to receive honor, not us. We want Him to be praised, not us. We want His love to be magnified, not ours.

Far too often in my life, though, my erroneous thoughts overshadow God. Sometimes I think too much of my ability to accomplish good things and change lives, and sometimes I'm so selfish that don't even care about changing lives. I just want to be happy and entertained.

> But it's not just my wrong thoughts about God that overshadow Him—it's also the absence of thoughts about Him.

When I don't care enough to even consider what God wants, my will, my desires, and my ambitions overshadow God in my life. God has given us the best sources of faith imaginable: the wonders of nature and the truth of His Word. General revelation in the natural world causes all people to sit up and notice that somebody somewhere is far bigger than they are. And God's Word gives us the best and most accurate account of His character. As we study the incredible truth about God, we find that we can never find the depths of all of His truth. As Paul thought about the wonder of God's sovereignty and love, he exclaimed, "Oh, the depth of the riches both of the wisdom and knowledge of God! How unsearchable are His judgments and unfathomable His ways!" (Romans 11:33)

Augustine reminds us that God uses His wondrous truth to comfort us as well as to build our faith. He wrote that God "cares for His creatures through that truth, the mind should be cleansed so that it is able to see that light and to cling to it once it is seen."[16]

Until we are overshadowed, we, like Peter, insist on our own agendas. When God interrupts us and overshadows us, then, as Augustine said, we will cling to the light of His presence!

When we think of being overshadowed, it can sound oppressive. But being in the presence of God is anything but heavy, oppressive, and difficult. Yes, we have to admit that we aren't the center of the universe, but that ounce of humility results in tons of experience of the goodness and greatness of God. Spurgeon commented, "He made men feel that they were poor, so that they might be willing to be made rich by His grace. He made them feel weary and burdened, so that they might come to Him for rest."[17]

To be honest, I really wanted to be an integral part of leading my dad to Christ. I had done a lot to get ready for that moment. I had prayed for him, visited him when others wouldn't, painted his house to show him I loved him, called him on the phone, and talked to him about Christ numerous times. And after all, I'm an evangelist! Surely I should have the honor of leading my own father to Christ!

But God overshadowed me, and I don't mind a bit! God accomplished His work in my father's heart, and that means far more to me than anything else. God overshadowed Joel, my dad's neighbors, and everybody else who had ever cared about him. God allowed us all to be a part of the process, but ultimately, it was God alone who worked to soften the hard heart of a man who didn't care about God at all. It was God's matchless grace that overshadowed us all.

Do you want to go to the mountain? Are you willing to be overshadowed?

Think about it . . .

1. Is being overshadowed by God attractive or threatening to you? Explain your answer.

2. Do we have to choose to be overshadowed, or can God do it regardless of what we do? Can you give examples of both?

3. Read Romans 11:33. In what way is this an expression of someone who is gladly overshadowed?

4. What are some ways your life would change if you were overshadowed by God's greatness and majesty?

"A VOICE came
out of the cloud . . ."

A bullet train.

Have you ever been on one? It's an incredible experience. Bullet trains were developed in Japan and Europe as mass transportation. I've got to tell you, they're a lot more fun than a bus! Not long ago, I was on a bullet train in Germany, traveling through the beautiful German countryside from Hamburg to Berlin. I had spoken in Hamburg with Kelly Green, a dear brother in the Lord and someone God used to help me early in my ministry. I owe a great deal to Kelly and his wife Beth for believing in what God was doing in me. When others said, "Thomas,

I'm not so sure about you," Kelly saw potential in me, encouraged me, and poured himself into me. His giving heart is combined with a rare and valuable trait: integrity.

I boarded the train in Hamburg with two friends. Ken is a worship pastor from Chattanooga, and Jay is a pastor in Stuttgart, Germany. I was excited about being in Germany to minister, but to be honest, I was equally excited about riding on a bullet train! I love speed, so I was thrilled to be in for the ride of my life.

The train left the Hamburg station, and while it went through the city, the speed remained quite modest. When we hit the edge of town, though, the train started picking up the pace. A monitor in each car informs passengers of the speed. My eyes bounced back and forth from looking at the outside scenery to the inside monitor. The monitor posted the speed in kilometers, so I had to do quick calculations every few minutes.

Soon we were at maximum speed: 180 miles per hour! And we cruised along smoothly for a while. As you can imagine, for three guys in our situation, the only other thing more interesting than speed was food. We walked forward to the dining car to eat breakfast. While we were eating, I kept looking out the window. As I viewed the hillside and the thousands of acres of beautiful farmland, it didn't seem as if we were going that fast. As a matter of fact, the train was so smooth that we had very little sense of our speed.

I had been looking at farms and houses in the distance because there was very little to see in close proximity to the train. But then objects began to appear closer to the train: telephone polls, signs along the track, and trees. That's when my perspective changed. Things in the distance had been easy to observe, but not those things next to the train. It was hard to pick out individual objects at that speed, but I tried my best. (I almost went cross-eyed, but that's a small price to pay for spiritual insight!)

Finally, I could sense we were going 180 miles per hour! With my new reference point, things I hadn't even seen before became important. From this perspective I had a completely different feeling about our speed. It seemed like we were flying!

Matthew continues his story about Jesus and His three friends on the mountain. A cloud had overshadowed them, and now, a voice boomed out of the silence. Matthew tells us a voice came out of the cloud and said, "This is My beloved Son, with whom I am well pleased."

God's voice is clear, loud, and audible. We know the guys heard and understood because they responded the way people react when they encounter God: They fell on their faces in awe! Why did God speak audibly to this group of men, and why did He say what He said?

The reference point for me on that bullet train was all of the things close to the train. Looking at them gave me a far more accurate perspective of the speed we were traveling. The reference point for Peter, James, and John was the booming voice of Almighty God.

When God reveals His glory, we must keep Him as the **reference point** in the encounter and not the encounter itself!

When you and I go to the mountain, our reference point isn't our goals, our needs, or our hopes and dreams. It's God. The first line of Rick Warren's bestseller, *The Purpose Driven Life* (Zondervan), is, "It's not about you." He's right. The Christian life isn't about you and me. It's about God. He's the one who loves, forgives, and reigns over the universe. We pray for His kingdom to come, not ours. We pray for wisdom to follow His will, not for Him to help us carry out our selfish goals. I lost track of the speed of the train when I stared off in the distance, and I learned I need to stay on track spiritually by keeping my eyes on the nearness and greatness of God.

As I read the Scriptures, I find that when God's voice is heard, He is authenticating a person or a message. At the baptism of Jesus, God's voice spoke to those present. On the mountain and out of the cloud, the Father used the same message to put His stamp of approval on His Son, Jesus Christ.

Can you imagine the scene? Three guys hike up a mountain with Jesus. Suddenly, His appearance is transformed. He's glowing! And two of the most revered men of God in all of history suddenly appear in front of them. A bright cloud forms overhead, and the booming voice of God thunders to tell them that this man they've been following is indeed the Son of God. Wow! No wonder they fell to the ground!

I'm sure Peter, James, and John never forgot the words, "This is My beloved Son, with whom I am well pleased." Later, after Jesus was raised from the dead and ascended to heaven, those men would experience severe persecution. They needed to remember whom they were serving and that the price they were paying was worth it. The message from the Father reminded them that they needed to be faithful to what they had seen and heard on the mountain that day.

In that breathtaking event, God revealed His nature in several ways. The men who listened and saw would never be the same. More than ever before, they realized that nothing, literally nothing, was more valuable and real than God Himself. I like the way John Piper stated this truth in a sermon several years ago: "God is ultimate reality, and beyond which, there is only more of God."

On the journey to the mountain, we need to hear from God. He probably won't appear in a cloud and speak in an audible voice, but He will remind us of passages of Scripture and impress our hearts with His desires. As God increasingly becomes the center of our lives, He will be the reference point for all of our decisions. His purposes will mean more than any of our own, and He will give us a glimpse into His heart for people. As we follow Him, we'll trust Him through the good times and the bad because we trust that He will use the mountain and the valley to shape us into the people He wants us to be. After all, it's all about Him.

Do you want to go to the mountain where God Himself is our reference point?

Think about it . . .

1. What's the fastest you've ever traveled (car, plane, train, boat)? Did you have a sense of how fast you were going? Why or why not?

2. Why do you think God felt the need to speak audibly on the mountain? Wasn't the rest of the scene enough to convince the three disciples?

3. How do you think it helped Peter, James, and John later in their lives to remember God's voice on the mountain that day?

4. What are some ways God speaks to you? How can you know each one is really God (and not last night's pizza, your selfish desires, or pressure from someone else)?

"LISTEN to Him!"

Could this be God?

About a year after I became a follower of Christ, a group of college friends and I wanted to spend our spring break sharing the gospel with other college students. We thought it would be lots of fun. A couple of friends were from Arizona, so we packed up and headed west with them. They even arranged a couple of large rallies where we could give our testimonies and tell people about the love of God.

I prayed and prepared for this trip like never before. I spent hours alone praying and reading the Bible. I wanted to be so in tune with God that He flowed out of me. We would probably find some opposition, so I wanted to be ready.

We arrived in Tucson at the University of Arizona. Besides the rallies, we split up in teams during the day and spread out over the campus to talk to as many people as possible. We had heard that the university had been chosen as the number one "party school" in America. What better place could there be to tell people about Jesus!

One day we were walking around a part of the campus where lots of students hang out. It was a beautiful area, and we found hundreds of students sitting on blankets, talking and studying. I approached a cluster of them with confidence that God had sent me to share His name, fame, glory, and gospel with them. It was a great experience! In one of the conversations, I talked with a pre-med student about the existence of God. (I had recently taken a Philosophy of Religion class, and I had acquired just enough knowledge to be dangerous!) All of my conversations that day reminded me again and again that I was totally dependent on God to work in people's lives. I just wanted to be faithful and follow Him.

After a full day of talking with individuals, small groups of people, and at the big rally that night, I was exhausted. And to be honest, I was so tired that I became very discouraged. At 1:00 or 2:00 in the morning, I drove to a restaurant. I hadn't eaten all day, and I was famished. As I sat at a booth, I overheard two ladies at the next table. They were talking about Jesus! I leaned over and told them that I was a Christian and couldn't help but be touched by their conversation about Jesus. They asked me sit with them. I told them I was discouraged because I had spent all day sharing the gospel, and I was drained physically and spiritually. I explained I had spent much time trying to stay in tune with God, but now I wondered what I was doing in Arizona. One of the ladies kindly asked me, "Thomas, do you mind if we lay hands on you and pray for you?"

I was thrilled by their kindness, and I replied, "No, not at all!" Those dear ladies prayed for me, and I sensed that God was refreshing me by their wonderful, encouraging prayers. I left the restaurant filled with food and filled with Him!

When I got to the car, I noticed a grocery store nearby. For some strange reason, I felt drawn to go inside. I thought, *This is really weird. Why do I feel like I need to go in there? Is this you, God?* I had asked that question dozens of times before. Again, I couldn't tell if the prompting was from God or just some random thought. I decided to respond anyway, and I walked through the front door of the grocery store. It looked empty. I didn't even see anyone at the checkout counter. It was so odd. I wondered, *What in the world am I doing in this store?*

I walked up an aisle. Nobody there. I turned the corner and saw a woman at the far end of the next aisle. Her eyes met mine. She was staring at me with a look of discouragement—the same look I'd had on my face an hour before. Suddenly, I realized why I was there. I walked toward her, but I could tell she thought this was just as awkward as I did! As I reached her, the words just flew out of my mouth: "I came here all the way from Oklahoma to tell you that God has not forgotten about you. He's real, and He loves you!"

She began to cry. She looked at me and said, "You have no idea how much I needed to hear that! My husband came home today and told me he was leaving me. I lost my job today, too. My husband took our kids with him tonight. I couldn't sleep, so I drove to the store." She paused a second, put her head down, and then told me, "I've been thinking about killing myself. I sat in the car before I came in, and I told God that if He was real and if He loved me, I needed Him to let me know."

In that moment, she was changed. But also, I was changed, and God was glorified. God had invited me to join Him. He spoke to me in the desire to go to Arizona, in the enthusiasm of my friends who came along, in the dear ladies who prayed for me, and in impressing me to go to that grocery store so late at night. God had a plan, and I just joined the journey to the mountain to hear His voice.

God wanted to be understood, so He made His voice crystal clear on the mountain with Jesus, Moses, Elijah, Peter, James, and John. If we want to go to the mountain, we must be willing to listen and respond. Peter was interrupted, the three men were overshadowed, and the voice spoke to get their attention and impart a message. Jesus was there, and the Father told the others, "Listen to Him!"

GOD WANTED TO BE SEEN, AND GOD WANTED TO BE HEARD!

To listen is to be sensitive to God's voice and His leading. There are no coincidences or accidents. Every person we meet and every situation we encounter are opportunities for God to speak to us and lead us. Author Dallas Willard says we live in a "God-saturated world." He is always at work, always present, always speaking. We just need to be attentive and listen. On the journey up the mountain, God is creating opportunities for us to be aware of Him. Will we pay attention?

He is setting up encounters along the path to and from the mountain to speak to us or through us!

Today a lot of people think they hear the voice of God, but I'm afraid many of them are listening to other voices. The primary way God speaks to you and me is through His Word. To be led by God, we need to immerse our minds and hearts in the truths of Scripture. Yes, it's a challenge, but we're digging for treasure worth more than anything in this world. Sometimes we hit a rich vein and insights flood our lives, but other times we find only enough flecks of gold to keep us going. We need to remember that God's purpose for us is always to build our faith. That's what pleases Him. He builds our faith in many ways, using many differing circumstances. All of them are tools He uses to craft us.

My favorite preacher is Jonathan Edwards, who lived in the early and middle 18th century. Edwards was convinced that God sometimes amazes us with His love and power, and sometimes He humbles us so we will trust Him more. He observed, " . . . that God, in the revelation of himself that he has made of himself to the world by Jesus Christ, has taken care to give a proportional manifestation of two kinds of excellencies or perfections of his nature, viz. those that especially tend to possess us with awe and reverence, and to search and humble us; and those that tend to win, to draw and encourage us."[18]

The revelation of God on the mountain first awed the three men (so much that they fell on their faces), but it also drew them to Jesus. Later, in the heat of persecution after Jesus ascended, those men stood strong because they trusted that Jesus was with them to the end of the world. He had awed them, and He had drawn them to Himself.

As I think about the three disciples who accompanied Jesus to the mountain and heard the voice of God that day, I can imagine that they never listened quite the same way again. Every time it thundered, every time the wind blew, and every time they heard waves crash on the shore, their ears probably perked up. And perhaps that heightened awareness carried over into the rest of their walks with God to make them more sensitive to His leading.

I thank God for that experience in Arizona years ago. That's where I began to learn to be sensitive to His voice. I'm still learning. In fact, I still have a lot to learn about being attentive to God's voice. But at least now I'm looking for Him and listening for Him. Now I believe He will remind me of a passage of Scripture just when I need it or direct me to take steps of faith even when those steps seem weird. Whether through His Word, in a circumstance, through another person, or through prompting from the Holy Spirit, God wants to speak to you and me.

Do you hear Him saying, "Do you want to go to the mountain?"

Think about it . . .

1. When was the last time God reminded you of a passage of Scripture just when you needed it? How did you respond?

2. What are some ways you can tell if an impression is from God?

3. In what way does the revelation of the greatness and grace of God's glory awe you, and in what way does it draw you to Him?

4. Who do you know who is most attentive to the leading of God? Describe the impact that ability has on that person's life and ministry.

"And when they HEARD this . . . they. . . were TERRIFIED"

13

I was terrified.

When I was young, my parents often went to another couple's house to play dominoes or cards late into the evening. My sister and I would play with their three kids. When it was finally time to go home, we usually had fallen asleep, so they carried us to the car. One night the twenty-minute ride home terrified me.

Just before leaving our friends' house, we heard a news bulletin announcing that a nearby family had been shot in their home. (Later we learned that two men had come to their door in rural Oklahoma pretending to be in need of help. The family graciously offered assistance, but the men had shot the father, the mother, and their two children. The parents both died of their wounds, but the children miraculously survived.) The news bulletin warned the community that the suspects were still at large. They could be hiding anywhere—including our house!

My parents knew of the man and woman who had been murdered.

As we drove home, all of us worried what we'd find. When we pulled into the driveway, my dad told all of us to stay in the car. From under his car seat, he pulled out a gun and a flashlight. He carefully opened the door and disappeared into the dark house. We all watched his flashlight shine through the windows of our home as he searched each room. Finally, when he was sure it was safe, he waved to us, and we went inside. I never had another good night's sleep there again. I was terrified.

A few months after that terrible night, an incident occurred at our home. My bedroom was at the front of our house. From my bed, I could see the front door. My parents' room was in the very back of the house. At about 2:00 in the morning, I saw a flashlight shining through the window of our front door. I was terrified.

I ran past the door, hoping whoever was out there wouldn't see me. I woke my dad and told him a stranger was trying to get in through the front door. He grabbed his pistol, went to the door, turned on the outside light, and saw two men. Dad yelled, "What do you want?"

One of them explained that their car had broken down and they needed to come in and use the phone. My dad told them he would call someone for them, but he wasn't going to let them in. At that point, one of the men began to open the screen door. My dad growled that he had a gun pointed at them and he'd shoot them if they tried to open the door any further. He told them to back off. And they did.

A few seconds later, we heard them start their car and drive away. Again, I was terrified.

Years later my parents divorced. At one point, I was still living in that house out in the middle of nowhere with my mom and my sister. When my dad moved out, he told me to keep my rifle loaded under my bed. I did, but I was still scared.

Fear is not always cowardice. It can be a perfectly reasonable response to a threat or an overwhelming circumstance. That's exactly what I experienced after one family was murdered and then men tried to break into our house. And it's what Peter, James, and John faced on the mountain when they saw Jesus transfigured, the cloud overshadow them, and the voice thunder above them. Matthew tells us, "And when the disciples heard this, they fell on their faces and were much afraid."

In our culture, many of us like to think of God as a buddy, a Santa Claus, or a warm blanket. We expect (and maybe demand) that He give us what we want and make us feel good. That's His job, isn't it? No, not exactly! A good and healthy relationship with God involves awe, respect, and reverence. That's what the Bible calls "fear." In fact, we don't grow much at all if we don't have a strong, healthy reverence for God. The psalmist wrote, "The fear of the Lord is the beginning of wisdom" (Psalm 111:10).

Throughout the pages of the Bible, when men and women encountered God or even had great thoughts about God, they responded with humility and wonder. God, they realized, is far bigger, far more powerful, and far smarter than they ever imagined. With the word of His mouth He created the universe, and with His word, He rules it now. We are atoms on a speck of dust revolving around a speck of a star in the incredibly vast ocean of God's creation. And He loves us.

When we passionately pursue Him and His glory, we'll long for Him like the deer panting for the water. When we find Him, we'll tremble in awe. On the mountain that day, God didn't protect those men from fear. He caused them to fear! God spoke with such authority that it was a natural reaction for the three men to experience fear.

Having a moment before God when He does something unforgettable produces in us a deeper understanding of His character and His call. He didn't speak from the cloud and tell them to listen in order to make them run and hide. Instead, God wanted to create a holy awareness of His awesome character so they would want to know Him more. They needed to get beyond curiosity and experience majesty.

God wants us to fall down to our knees before Him in awe, wonder, and reverence. This is not a frequent reaction to the Lord these days. Notice, however, that even though the disciples had fallen down in fear, Jesus didn't want them to continue to be afraid. Having the fear of God and being continually afraid are two different things. The Bible tells us, "God has not given us a spirit of fear, but of power, love, and self-control" (2 Timothy 1:7, ESV).

> Having a moment before God when He does something unforgettable can arouse a deeper understanding of His awesome power that causes us to be more attentive to the call of His voice!

Jonathan Edwards had a clear understanding of our need to be gripped with the fear of God. He wrote, "The Scriptures place much of religion in godly fear; insomuch that an experience of it is often spoken of as the character of those who are truly religious persons. They tremble at God's Word, they fear before Him, their flesh trembles for fear of Him, they are afraid of His judgments, His excellency makes them afraid, and His dread falls upon them."[19]

Complacency, apathy, boredom. Those are the traits of many believers today. Far too often, we have very little loyalty to God because we aren't amazed by Him. Godly fear produces heartfelt worship, obedience, tenacity, and conviction. We are too easily satisfied with "feel good" messages and entertaining songs. God isn't a Santa Claus, and He's not a "specially attentive waiter" we tip when He pleases us. We need a few men and women who aren't satisfied with anything less than an encounter with the Almighty so that they are changed forever. To encounter Him is to be amazed, and to be amazed is to worship.

MANY WHO ARE CURIOUS ARE NOT CALLED.

The three men on the mountain fell "face down." They felt abject humility in the presence of God. When we fall down before God, He draws near to us (James 4:8-10). We see His character and His purposes more clearly, and we become receptive to His leading in our lives.

When was the last time you fell face down before God in a posture of humility? I believe this is a frequently missing element in our pursuit of intimacy with God. If you want to go to the mountain, you'll have to bow down.

Remember that Jesus didn't take everybody to the mountain. He picked three of His men, and they made their hearts ready for the trip. Their preparation probably included many times of listening to Jesus on their travels, responding to Him in faith (or at least by asking some questions), and continuing to follow Him day after day.

The willingness to obey is a vital element in our spiritual lives. Here, many of us end our journey prematurely. We realize God may be leading us somewhere we don't want to go, so we bail out. Our faith in His goodness and wisdom isn't strong enough for us to take the hard but necessary step to continue with Him.

John Calvin was a lion of the faith. His study of God's Word has transformed the minds of Christians for centuries. But Calvin wasn't a bland academic. His faith was strong, and his commitment was powerful. He wrote: "In coming into the presence of God, we cannot look for acceptance unless we bring to his service a willing mind."[20]

I was terrified. I should have been. Murderers shot a whole family near my home, and those two men later came to our door. Wouldn't you be afraid? Fear isn't always a bad thing. Sometimes it causes us to shrink back from courage and action, yet fear is a good and right response to something so amazing, so incredible, so wonderful that we can hardly comprehend it. On the mountain, that's what Peter, James, and John discovered. Will you and I discover that same truth?

Do you want to find wonder, amazement, and awe on the mountain?

Think about it . . .

1. Describe a time when you've been really afraid. What did you want to do? Was it a reasonable fear of a real threat, or was it irrational fear?

---

2. Describe a time when you've been most amazed at the greatness and goodness of God. What did that experience make you want to do?

3. What are the similarities and differences in the two ways we can experience fear?

4. Do you want to have the kind of fear of God that the three men had on the mountain? Why or why not?

"and Jesus came to them and He TOUCHED them."

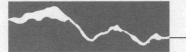

14

He wanted to

use it to change me.

I was adopted as an infant. My mom and dad loved me—there's no doubt about that. I grew close to my mom, to "Grams" (my grandmother), and to my Uncle Bill. I loved them very much, and I still do. They were all wonderful to me.

But a storm was brewing at home. My parents hated each other. They yelled, screamed, and fought. When my dad wasn't home, my mom told me how much she hated him. And when my dad talked to me in private, he told me how much he despised my mom. Finally, after years of bitterness, they divorced. But that wasn't the end of it. They fought an intense custody battle for me.

Even though the court awarded me to my mom, I went to live with my dad. For the first time in my life, he was kind to me. He didn't ignore me any longer. He loved me, he bought me things, and he promised it would be this way even though my mom had warned me that his custody was temporary. She warned me that my dad would return to his old, painful ways.

My dad eventually remarried and indeed, my mother was a prophet—he returned to his old ways. When I entered high school, the years of hurt had taken their toll. I felt empty, miserable, lonely, and above all, lost. Some friends invited me to go to church, and I began to attend occasionally. I soon discovered that to be "in" I needed to join the church and "make a profession of faith." Soon I walked down the aisle and was baptized.

But I still felt empty, and the pain was more piercing than ever. I looked to the church for answers, but all I found was more questions. Then I noticed that many students there led quite a different life on Sunday than they lived the rest of the week. The people who brought me to church partied with me on the weekend, which was discouraging and confusing. Of course, not everybody was a hypocrite. Many of them reached out to me and showed me love. They introduced me to Jesus. But I just couldn't get past the hurt in my heart and the inconsistency of the lives of some people.

At home, we had a large liquor cabinet full of all kinds of alcohol. I learned early in my life that drinking would temporarily drown the pain. And I liked it! I got hooked. In fact, I thought I'd found exactly what I was looking for! I drank before I went to school and sometimes in my car after school was out. I usually drank in private because I didn't want to tarnish my "wholesome kid" façade. I pretended to be cool and macho, but that was just a mask to help me fit in. I was utterly empty and tragically lost.

One night during my senior year, my dad and his third wife, my stepmom, were fighting. I had heard this type of fighting for years, but this time I had had enough. It was late and I was already in bed. I jumped up, ran into the living room, and yelled, "Dad, would you please stop? I can't take this anymore!"

My dad pointed his finger at me, and with a glare on his face I'll never forget, he said, "Get the heck [actually, he used another word] out of my house, and don't come back. I'm not your dad anymore!"

I left and moved in with a friend who had a wonderful family. After a while, I wore out my welcome, but some other families took me in. I stayed away until my dad demanded I move back in because I was 17 and he was "still legally responsible" for me.

After I graduated from high school, a child psychologist met with me and reported that I was in the beginning stages of becoming an alcoholic. I didn't care. I needed some relief from the constant pain, and alcohol made me numb.

I went off to college with $1,800 in the bank. My tuition, room, board, and books were already paid for. I had saved money for extra expenses, but I spent most of it in the first couple of months, mostly on booze. I was miserable.

One night I was drunk in the dorm. I flew into rage and punched the window in our hall. The impact broke out a huge section of the plate glass, and it crashed from the sixth floor to the sidewalk outside the building. My friends who were standing next to me immediately ran to their rooms.

A few weeks later, I was at the end of my rope. I felt that no one cared about me. In my despair, I decided to leave school. We had two more weeks of classes before Christmas break, but I couldn't go another day. I didn't want to flunk out, so I went to my professors and begged them to give me my tests early. They agreed, so I took the exams in their offices and left school without telling anyone.

But I had nowhere to go. My friends were still at college, so I couldn't stay with them. I met a girl named Carrie at a bar. She lived in a little town about an hour from my house. I quickly devised a plan to stay with her until Christmas break and then ask my dad if I could move back in with him. But Carrie was just as miserable as I was. She asked the same questions I was asking—questions that seemed to have no answers. I didn't want to stay with someone as hopeless and hurting as I was, so at about 2:00 A.M., I drove in a pouring rainstorm to my dad's house.

When I arrived, I knew he would be furious if I woke him in the middle of the night after leaving school two weeks early, so I slept in my car in the driveway. At dawn I went into the house, greeted my dad, and then stayed in my old room most of the day. In the late afternoon, my dad asked me to take a shotgun to his friend Mark, who was going hunting and wanted to borrow it. My dad put the gun and a dufflebag of shotgun shells into my car and gave me directions to Mark's house.

Mark lived on a ranch about ten miles away. On the way, the years of shame and guilt whirled like a tornado in my mind. I had messed up everything I had ever tried to do, and I felt as though nobody cared about me at all. I was weeping . . . frantic . . . hopeless. I began to cry uncontrollably. I veered over to the shoulder of the road and pulled the gun out of the case. I loaded a shell into the chamber and put the barrel up to my face. My only thought was, *I'm going to blow my head off, and no one will care that I'm gone!*

I took a deep breath, and I realized that death is permanent. The fact that I had gone that far scared me. I slowly placed the gun back in its case, put the car in gear, and delivered the gun to Mark. When he walked out to my car, he could tell I had been crying. He asked, "Thomas, what's wrong?"

I told him I wanted to be left alone, so he took the gun and walked back into his house. As I drove down his long gravel driveway to the dirt road at the bottom of the hill, a name flashed in my head like a neon sign: Diane. She had been like a mom to me in high school. Her daughter was one of my best friends, and every time I showed up at church, Diane had an encouraging word for me. She was always glad to see me—that meant a lot. She lived very near Mark's house.

I pulled into Diane's driveway hoping she was home. When I looked at my clock on the car radio, it was 7:01 P.M. on Wednesday—time for the midweek service at church. Dang. She wouldn't be home. But then I saw her car, and I was excited. If anyone could help me, it was her.

I knocked on the door, and it immediately flew open. It was like she was standing at the door waiting for me, yet the expression on her face told me she was puzzled. She asked, "Thomas, what are you doing here?"

I told her I had gotten out of college early. She asked me why, and I gave her a lame answer. Actually, the best answer I could think of was, "I don't know."

She frowned, "You've gotten out of school early, and you don't know why." (It was more of a question than a statement.) I told her about taking the tests early and that no one knew I was home. The look on her face got my attention. It was like she knew something I didn't know. She asked me to come in.

I sat down on the couch, and she sat in a chair. I began to pour my heart out. Through my tears, I told her, "Nobody loves me. Nobody cares. I've tried church and religion. I have to drink to drown the pain. I tell you, *nobody loves me!*"

She looked at me and spoke with compassion, "Thomas Young, shut up and don't ever say that again!" She reminded me that my mom, my grandma, my Uncle Bill, and she loved me. But the pain of my childhood and my dumb choices blinded me from seeing their love.

Diane knew what was wrong. Jesus had never touched me. I needed His love and forgiveness. I was miserable because I was lost, helpless and hopeless apart from God. I desperately needed His love, His forgiveness, and His healing touch.

Diane opened her Bible to Romans 5:8. She read, "God demonstrates His own love toward us, in that while we were yet sinners, Christ died for us." She said that sin deserves death, and she shared how Jesus died on the cross to pay the penalty for my sin. Christ actually took my sins on Himself on the cross to pay for them so I could be forgiven. He was dying . . . for me!

Diane handed the Bible to me and said, "Read it for yourself." I began to read, but she stopped me and said, "Put your name in the verse wherever you see a pronoun."

I read it this way: "God demonstrated His own love toward Thomas in that while Thomas was a sinner, Christ died for Thomas." Wow! Right there in Diane's living room, God touched me. I heard Him call to me that He wanted to give me a new life. Then that radical moment culminated with an insight of what God was doing.

Diane had a smirk on her face—the same one she had when she came to the door. Her expression indicated she knew something I didn't. She said, "You know, it's Wednesday night, and we always go to church. I actually drove to church a little while ago, but the Lord told me to get back in my car and drive home. Then He told me to wait. I've been sitting here wondering why I was here—until I saw you!"

Wow. I didn't tell anybody I was coming home a couple of weeks early from school. I didn't even know why I took those tests early and left college. Certainly nobody knew my dad would send me on an errand to Diane's neighbor, and I hadn't thought of Diane at all until I left Mark's house.

AT THAT MOMENT, I REALIZED GOD HAD SET ME UP SO HE COULD TOUCH MY HEART AND CHANGE MY LIFE!

Matthew described Jesus' actions when His three followers were blown away by the presence of God on the mountain. He wrote, "And Jesus came to them and touched them and said, 'Arise, and do not be afraid.'"

Simple and profound—Jesus touched them. They were terrified, in need and confused, and Jesus stepped toward them, reached out His hand, and touched them. They needed to become sure of God. Jesus was leading them with a touch. It was that touch that created a deeper desire to follow Him.

Dietrich Bonhoeffer discovered the beauty of experiencing the power of God in being touched by Him. He said, "I am sure of God's hand and guidance. . . . You must never doubt that I am thankful and glad to go the way which I am being led. My past life is abundantly full of God's mercy, and above all sin stands the forgiving love of the Crucified."[21]

Life is tough. The road to seeing and hearing God is a difficult journey. In order to stay on the path of intimacy with Him, you'll have to be convinced—thoroughly, absolutely, overwhelmingly convinced—that Jesus Christ is your Lord and Savior. Your conversion experience may have happened a long time ago, or it may have happened two minutes ago when you read my story. No matter how long ago it was, that moment is crucial to your climb up the mountain.

If it remains a wonder that God would choose to forgive you, then you'll remain sensitive to Him. But if it becomes an old bore, it's easy to slide into complacency and indifference. Because of our sins, you and I deserve to be "where the worm does not die and the fire is not quenched." But in God's magnificent grace, He has rescued us from eternal destruction. In addition, He calls us His own dearly beloved children and gives us wonderful gifts to enjoy. No, our salvation isn't a bore. It remains the most thrilling thing that will ever happen to us! And it's the foundation of our spiritual growth.

Peter knew a thing or two about the transforming power of forgiveness. In his second letter, he gave a progression of traits that signify spiritual growth. He wrote: "Now for this very reason also, applying all diligence, in your faith supply moral excellence, and in your moral excellence, knowledge; and in your knowledge, self-control, and in your self-control, perseverance, and in your perseverance, godliness; and in your godliness, brotherly kindness, and in your brotherly kindness, love. For if these qualities are yours and are increasing, they render you neither useless nor unfruitful in the true knowledge of our Lord Jesus Christ" (2 Peter 1:5-8).

Peter then explains that there's one single motivation for continuing on the path of growth: "For he who lacks these qualities is blind or shortsighted, having forgotten his purification from his former sins" (2 Peter 1:9).

And finally, Peter encourages us to let the piercing memory of our salvation keep us on the path of loving and obeying Christ. He wrote, "Therefore, brethren, be all the more diligent to make certain about His calling and choosing you; for as long as you practice these things, you will never stumble" (2 Peter 1:10).

God wants to touch you. It's His touch alone that changes lives. Some church leaders believe they need new, fancy techniques or technology so that people can be touched. The Bible teaches us that hearts are changed "not by might nor by power, but by [God's] Spirit" (Zechariah 4:6). When God touches our lives, complacency is shattered by the power of His love, and apathy melts away in the fire of His purposes. Instead of only knowing about God, we really know Him.

God Himself initiates this healing touch. Notice that the passage says, "And Jesus came to them." Jesus initiated the contact with the three men. The events of the past moments—the transfiguration, the cloud, and the voice—set them up for the touch of God. Yes, they were set up by God!

Some of us might say, "Well, God hasn't initiated anything with me! I sure don't see Him making any effort." But He has. The greatest evidence of God's initiative is the cross. Jesus came to earth and died. Jesus rose from the grave on the third day. Jesus made sure that what was needed would be provided through His cross. While we did nothing, He did everything. He decided to condescend to us so that that we could ascend to Him. God has taken the initiative, even after we have walked away from Him (Isaiah 53:6; Romans 5:8). We can go to the mountain because He made the first step toward us. He came!

Jesus told the three disciples, "Get up. Do not be afraid." Was Jesus contradicting the impact of the Father on these men? Certainly not. Jesus was saying,

> ## "I don't want you to be *afraid* of Me;
> ## I want you to be in *awe* of Me."

We find here again the blend of greatness and grace, of tenderness and tenacity, of power and kindness. God revealed Himself with such diversity that it caused them to see Jesus and respond to Him in the way God desired.

Missionary Jim Elliot was gripped with a sense of God's forgiveness, and it compelled him to pray boldly that God's grace would transform his life. In his journal, he wrote his prayer: "Father, let me be weak that I might loose my clutch on everything temporal. My life, my reputation, my possessions, Lord, let me loose the tension of the grasping hand. Even, Father, I would lose the love of *fondling*. How often I have released a grasp only to retain what I prized by 'harmless' longing, the fondling touch. Rather, open my hand to receive the nail of Calvary, as Christ's was opened—that I, releasing all, might be released, unleashed from all that binds me now."[22]

God's majesty and kindness are shown in this event on the mountain. We find His transcendence—that He is "far above all"—in Jesus' glowing countenance, the brilliance of the cloud, and the sound of His voice. But that's not all God is. The all-powerful God is also the one who reaches out and touches those He loves in kindness and reassurance. We desperately need to believe He has all of these qualities so that we are in awe of His power and we are attracted to His love.

On the mountain, we'll find a kind and awesome God. Do you want to go there?

Think about it . . .

1. Describe what God has done to "touch" you.

2. When you pray, do you think more about the awesome power of God, or His kindness? How does your mindset affect your expectations of His answers to your prayers?

3. Read 2 Peter 1:5-11. Describe the importance of marveling that God has saved you, forgives you, and loves you.

4. What are some ways you can rivet those truths more deeply in your heart?

5. Reread Jim Elliot's prayer. Does it express your heart's desire? Explain your answer.

"and **LIFTING UP** their eyes they saw no one except Jesus"

15

They wanted to suppress God.

When the bullet train rolled into Berlin, a member of a local church took us on a tour of the city. He told us about Hitler and the Nazis, the obliteration of the city by Allied bombing, and the takeover of much of Germany by the Soviet forces after the war. As we walked along the streets of what used to be East Berlin, he showed us some murals on the sides of buildings—propaganda paintings depicting happiness and success under the communist regime.

Communism isn't just an economic program; it's a philosophy of life. A basic premise is that man can achieve total fulfillment on his own—without God. In fact, God is seen as "the opiate of the people," a hindrance to personal and economic success. Throughout the communist world, leaders tried to suppress the church and faith in God. But God won't allow man to suppress Him.

We turned a corner, and our German brother pointed to a huge tower in the middle of the city. This communications tower had been built by the communists as a statement to the West. Its enormous size proclaimed the dominance and power of communism. The tower could be seen for miles outside the city. Our guide smiled and explained that this symbol of godless philosophy backfired on the government. At certain times of the day, reflected sunlight created the image of a huge cross hovering over the city! The communist government had been furious. They made several attempts to change the tower to prevent the reflection, reconstructing and then repainting the top of the tower—but nothing worked. The cross still mysteriously appeared on the tower. The cross in Berlin simply could not be suppressed, no matter how hard they tried.

The cross of Christ is a dividing line. Some see it and embrace it; others see it and turn away in disgust. And to be honest, many of us may have become too familiar with it as a symbol. It should remind us that one of the most remarkable facts in all of history is that God became a human being and died as a criminal. Because of our sins, we deserved death . . . and that's exactly the price Christ paid. The sinless

Messiah paid the debt of sin, and we are set free. Does that make sense to you? It sure doesn't to everybody. Paul told us, "For the word of the cross is to those who are perishing foolishness, but to us who are being saved it is the power of God" (1 Cor. 1:18). To the lost, the meaning of the cross of Christ is hidden. Paul explained, "And even if our gospel is veiled, it is veiled to those who are perishing" (2 Cor. 4:3).

Eternal life is a gift from God, but before we receive that gift, God has to give us something else—the faith to believe in the first place. As sinners, we are "enemies" of God (James 4:4). We are without God and without hope in the world. We have nothing in us that causes us to long for God on our own. God must plant that longing in our hearts. Augustine called this longing "prevenient grace," the grace that comes before others. We need grace to see our need for Jesus before we can trust Him as Savior and learn to depend on Him each day.

After Jesus touched His terrified friends on the mountain to remind them that the awesome God is also the God of tenderness, Matthew tells us, "And lifting up their eyes they saw no one, except Jesus Himself alone." Peter, James, and John had seen something none of the rest of us will see until Jesus returns in the clouds in His radiant glory with His mighty angels at the Second Coming. The sight over-whelmed them! But Jesus touched them and said in effect, "Hey guys, I know you're blown away by the awesome sight you've seen, but don't be afraid. I love you." When they looked up, the cloud was gone, the voice had fallen silent, Moses and Elijah had disappeared, and Jesus wasn't glowing any more. All they saw was Jesus. Can you imagine how they looked at Him and at each other?

As I thought about this moment in the drama, it hit me that the three men saw Jesus most clearly when they were down. They had fallen to the ground in awe and humility. They were broken and vulnerable. They feared for their lives. They sensed their need more than ever—and Jesus touched them. Why is it important that they were down? Because when you are down you have to look up. It is when you are down that Jesus can be seen most clearly. When you fall down you will have to look up, and then you will see Him.

I hate being down. As a red-blooded American, I think I should always be on top of everything. I expect to win every game and every battle, but that's not God's plan. He gives us plenty of successes and victories, but He also gives us enough defeats to remind us that we desperately need Him. Those times of disappointment, frustration, and heartache are teachable moments.

THAT'S WHEN I'M MOST OPEN TO GOD'S DIRECTION, THAT'S WHEN I WANT TO BE TOUCHED BY JESUS, AND THAT'S WHEN GOD DELIGHTS IN SHOWING ME WHO HE IS.

Those times are precious to God because He accomplishes His primary purpose of getting my attention, revealing my vulnerabilities, and building my faith in Him. Maybe I should value those moments a bit more, too. At another time on another mountain, Jesus told His followers, "Blessed are the pure in heart, for they shall see God" (Matthew 5:8).

Our thoughts of God are sometimes scandalous! Some of us view Him as a genie in a bottle. We think we can rub the bottle (by going through some spiritual ritual), and God will magically give us whatever we want. Others see Him as an angry judge, ready to punish us for every mistake. Some see God as a kind but out-of-touch grandfather who is warm and loving but doesn't really know what's going on in our lives. Measured against the truths of the Scripture, these thoughts are truly scandalous!

Those who know the Bible find faith-building truths about both the transcendence and immanence of God. He is awesome in His power and might. I work up a sweat when I cut the grass, but with only a word, He created the entire universe. But God is also as near as our breath, as attentive as a loving mother, and as thoughtful as a best friend. These furious opposites about God need to remain furious and opposite, continuing to challenge our puny concepts of Him and to stretch our faith muscles.

A. W. Tozer challenges me to see God more clearly. He took no prisoners when he wrote, "The essence of idolatry is the entertainment of thoughts about God that are unworthy of Him."[23]

When our thoughts of God are too small, our faith becomes anemic, and our passion for Christ and His cause deteriorates into self-absorbed activities.

This is one of the great problems of our day.
Many of us have a chiseled view of God.
What we don't like is just chipped
and scaled away.

It is popular to have your own version of God. Our view of Him has been maligned, and that shallowness has spread through our churches like a cancer. For example, we talk a lot about the love of God, and rightly so. But the love and grace of God shine most brightly in light of God's righteous judgment of sin. Judgment must be real for grace to have significance. Like the showcase in a jewelry store, the sparkling diamonds of love and grace are demonstrated most clearly against the dark, dull background of sin and judgment.

I've heard people claim, "The Bible says, 'God is love,' and that's all I need to know about God." Really? Is that all God has revealed of Himself? Actually, there are four "God is" statements in the New Testament. Three of them are comforting: "God is love," "God is spirit," and "God is light." But the fourth one is also true: "God is a consuming fire." Yet above all of these "God is" statements is the greatest fact about Him: God *is*—period. Think of it. The greatest thing about God is that He is.

Others think of Jesus as always meek and mild. They feel more comfortable with His kindness, and they like to envision Him as the guy in the stained glass holding a lamb. But Jesus called those who rejected Him "a brood of vipers" and "whitewashed tombs." To those who demanded physical blessings from Him, He raised the stakes. Realizing His listeners would misunderstand and be repulsed, He told them they couldn't be disciples unless they ate His flesh and drank His blood (John 6:53). He told His followers that He hadn't come to bring peace, but a sword (Matthew 10:34). He said He longed for the day that the fire of judgment was kindled (Luke 12:49). Jesus always meek and mild? Hardly!

THE GOSPEL IS NOT FOR WIMPS.

Jesus Christ paid a horrible debt, and He expects us to appreciate all He has done to set us free. Paul described his heartfelt response to the gospel this way, "For the love of Christ controls us, having concluded this, that one died for all, therefore all died; and He died for all, that they who live should no longer live for themselves, but for Him who died and rose again on their behalf" (2 Cor. 5:14-15).

The love of God? Yes, of course. It's what draws us to Christ and motivates us to live for Him. How is His love shown to us? Not by empty sentimentalism, but by the bloody sacrifice of the cross to rescue us from hell and give us purpose, freedom, and real life. Tozer explained, "Low views of God destroy the gospel for all who hold them."[24]

One of my favorite passages in the Bible is Isaiah 40. This wonderful text depicts the greatness of God incredibly well. I often find a quiet place to read it. Why? Because I often need to be reminded of the greatness and grace of Almighty God. "Seeing" Jesus means that we go beyond our limited human concepts of Him that make us comfortable, and we embrace Him for who He really is. We marvel at His tenderness, but we also are amazed at His strength and toughness. Actually, we will never fully know Him as He is. We simply can't. Finite minds are unable to comprehend the infinite God, and in that realization, we marvel even more.

The experience of Jesus' three friends on the mountain gives us a glimpse of a life of faith. It's not comfortable! The more we grasp the transcendence of God, the sooner we fall down in abject humility because we are overwhelmed with His greatness. But then as we respond to His tender touch, we rise and see Him more clearly as one who loves us enough to die for us. I hope you and I can see more clearly how incomparable and indescribable He is.

> The more clearly we see Him, the more we'll respond with unbridled **attraction**, undaunted **attention**, and inexpressible **admiration**.

The communists couldn't suppress God in the minds of the people of Berlin. God has given all of humanity a tower to remind us that He is present, that He cares, and that He has the power to transform lives. That tower is the cross of Christ.

That's what we'll find on the mountain. Do you want to go?

Think about it . . .

1. What might be the result of thinking of Christ as *only* kind and tender? Or as *only* mighty and majestic?

2. Review this chapter's statements about the toughness of Jesus. How do they make you feel about Him . . . and about yourself?

3. Read Isaiah 40 twice. The first time, read straight through the passage. The second time, mark the verses that tell you about the greatness of God and those that tell you about His kindness.

4. How would it affect your life if you embraced all of God's "furious opposites" more fully?

DO you?

16

Life is a mission trip.

We began our journey with this statement, and we'll end with it. Life isn't about staying in our comfort zones, trying to protect ourselves from the risk of following Christ, and piling up as many possessions as possible. A life of faith is a rich, rewarding—and somewhat risky— journey of taking Jesus' hand and going with Him wherever He goes.

We must be careful to follow Jesus. It's a rewarding risk. But in the process of going to the mountain, there are many traps, snares, and distractions that threaten to diminish intimacy with God. Every day we must be mindful of the warning so clearly articulated by Dietrich Bonhoeffer: "The call of Jesus teaches us that our relation to the world has been built on an illusion."[25]

I'm convinced that we won't take Jesus' hand and go with Him unless we realize that all this life offers is ultimately empty. When we come to that conclusion (and many never do), we become desperate to fill the hole in our hearts. Desperation drives some to drugs, some to sex, some to climb the ladder of success, and some to Christ. A gnawing sense of need isn't the worst thing in the world. In fact, it's absolutely essential to a life of hope and faith. Oswald Chambers had a virile trust in God. He never shrank from the reality that God creates needs in our lives so we'll turn to Him. He wrote, "A sense of need is one of the greatest benedictions because it keeps our life rightly related to Jesus Christ."[26]

On the day when I was broken and frustrated, I knew something needed to change. I desperately needed God to reach into my heart, touch me deeply, heal my hurts, and give me new direction. I cried out to Him for help, and He led me to Matthew's account of the transfiguration. The insights God gave me in that study have been light and salt to me. I've marveled at God's kindness as He spoke His Word into my heart to heal and help in ways I never imagined. As I've shared these thoughts with people, I'm amazed that God would use my point of desperation to help others grasp His greatness, grace, and glory. God is, indeed, kind to me.

Throughout these pages, I've asked the same question over and over again: "Do you want to go to the mountain?" You've already answered that question. If you didn't want to go, you surely wouldn't still be reading this book! Let me give you a few final thoughts to keep you going. As you pour out your heart to God, He may take you to the mountain today, but He also may wait until "six days later" to take you. Of course, that represents an unspecified amount of time, so be patient. Yet be assured that God delights in your desire to know Him and follow Him. He will reveal Himself in the time, place, and method of His choosing.

GOD IS THE ONE WHO INITIATES THE JOURNEY AND TAKES YOU THERE.

You can't just charge up the mountain on your own! As you sense His leading, go with Him, but realize it's a journey. Hikes take time, and they require tenacity to keep going when we get tired or discouraged. God may meet you in a way that you never expected. Certainly, that was the case for Peter, James, and John. Don't go with any preconceived ideas of how God will speak to you. Let the Word of God soak into your heart and mind. God will use His truth to guide, affirm, refresh, and correct you. Paul told us, "Let the word of Christ richly dwell within you" (Col. 3:16). It dwells in us richly when we read, reflect, and ponder how biblical passages apply to our lives. Your mind and heart are a sponge, but it takes time for things to sink in. Be sure you carve out enough time to let God's magnificent truth sink deep into your heart.

Part of the process necessarily involves experiences of humility. When God shows you how sinful and small you are, don't despair. That prepares you to be touched by Jesus. It's worth it.

What now? Ask God to open your heart to the truth of your desperate needs and His gracious provisions. Ask Him to give you a deeper love for Him and the joy of obeying Him. When He prompts you to take a step, take it! That's the adventure of walking with Him. We won't always understand the reason for each prompting of His Spirit, but we must trust that He has His reasons.

As you climb the mountain, you'll experience both discontent and incredible fulfillment. Both responses draw us more closely to God. Let your appetite for God, His Word, and His calling cause you to grow stronger each day.

As we close this book, I want to leave you with a final comment from John Piper, who has clear insight into our purpose as God's children. In his book, *Seeing and Savoring Jesus Christ,* Piper concluded, "God made us to magnify his greatness—the way telescopes magnify stars. He created us to put his goodness and truth and beauty and wisdom and justice on display. The greatest display of God's glory comes from deep delight in all that he is. This means that God gets the praise and we get pleasure. God created us so that he is most glorified in us when we are most satisfied in him."[27]

Don't you think it's time that your life became a mission trip? I know you want to go to the mountain! So do I.

Won't you join me on going to the mountain?

endnotes

1   John Piper, *Seeing and Savoring Jesus Christ,* (Wheaton, Ill.: Cross-
    way Books, 2001), p. 16.

2   Hugh T. Kerr, *A Compendium of Luther's Theology* (Philadelphia:
    Westminster Press, 1943).

3   Randy Alcorn, *Grace and Truth* (Sisters, Ore.: Multnomah Pub-
    lishers, 2003), p. 37.

4   Cited by Philip Yancey, *Reaching for the Invisible God* (Grand Rap-
    ids: Zondervan, 2000), p. 221.

5   Richard Foster, *Celebration of Discipline* (New York: HarperCol-
    lins, 1998), p. 20.

6   Larry Crabb, *Finding God* (Grand Rapids: Zondervan, 1993),
    p. 18.

7   Charles H. Spurgeon, *God's Joy in Your Heart* (New Kensington,
    Pa.: Whitaker House Publishers, 1998), p. 148.

8   R. C. Sproul, *The Soul's Quest for God* (Phillipsburg, N.J.: P & R
    Publishing, reissued 2003), p. 5.

9   John Piper, *When I Don't Desire God* (Wheaton, Ill.: Crossway
    Books, 2004), p.31.

10 Richard Foster, *Celebration of Discipline* (New York: Harper Collins, 1978, 1988, 1998), p. 113.

11 Oswald Chambers, *Run Today's Race* (Grand Rapids: Discovery House Publishers, 1968).

12 David Hazard (compiler), *Early Will I Seek Thee* (Minneapolis: Bethany House Publishers, 1991), p. 69.

13 St. Augustine, *On Christian Doctrine* (Upper Saddle River, N.J.: Prentice Hall Press, 1958) p. 12.

14 Brother Lawrence, *Practicing the Presence of God* (Nashville: Upper Room Publishers, 1956), p. 22.

15 Charles H. Spurgeon, *Joy in Christ's Presence* (New Kensington, Pa.: Whitaker House Publishers, 1997), p. 23.

16 St. Augustine, *On Christian Doctrine* (Upper Saddle River, N.J.: Prentice Hall Press, 1958), p. 13.

17 Charles H. Spurgeon, *God Loves You* (New Kensington, Pa.: Whitaker House, 1997), p. 66.

18 *The Works of Jonathan Edwards,* Vol. 1, (Peabody, Mass.: Hendrickson Publishers, 1998), p. 412.

19 *The Works of Jonathan Edwards,* Vol. 1, (Peabody, Mass.: Hendrickson Publishers, 1998), p. 238.

20 John Calvin, *Commentary on the Psalms,* as quoted in *Heart Aflame* (Phillipsburg, N.J.: P & R Publishing [compiler], 1999), p. 138.

21 Dietrich Bonhoeffer, *Cost of Discipleship* (New York: The MacMillan Company, 1963), p. 17.

22 Elisabeth Elliot, *Shadow of the Almighty* (San Francisco: Harper-SanFrancisco, 1957), p. 59.

23 A. W. Tozer, *The Knowledge of the Holy* (San Francisco: Harper & Row, 1961), p. 11.

24 A. W. Tozer, *The Knowledge of the Holy* (San Francisco: Harper & Row, 1961), p. 11.

25 Dietrich Bonhoeffer, *Cost of Discipleship* (New York: The MacMillan Company, 1963), p. 80.

26 Oswald Chambers, *Prayer: A Holy Occupation* (Grand Rapids: Discovery House Publishers, 1993), p. 52.

27 John Piper, *Seeing and Savoring Jesus Christ* (Wheaton, Ill.: Crossway Books, 2004), p. 124.

about thomas young

Thomas Young's life is a story of the transforming power of God. He was adopted as an infant in Oklahoma City, Oklahoma, and he grew up in a dysfunctional family laced with brokenness and pain. The pain of his childhood left him on a desperate search for "real life." As an 18 year-old college student, he was told that he was an alcoholic. This sent him even further in to a tailspin of self-destruction. One night, with thoughts of suicide and with a gun in his hand, God led him to the greatest miracle of all: salvation through Jesus Christ! (Read Chapter 14 about that night.) Thomas was saved, and as he says, he has "never gotten over it!"

In his ministry called Young Endeavors, Thomas travels all over the world speaking about the wonder of God. He has been called the "God Talker" because of the emphasis in his messages about the incredible character of God and the magnificence of the gospel. One pastor said he is "theology on fire!" Thomas's clear articulation of the gospel, passionate style, and straight-from-the-Word approach keep him on the road speaking at churches, conferences, and events all over the world.

Thomas is married to Erin, whom he says is "the most incredible follower of Christ I know." Thomas and Erin have three children: Morgan, Graham, and Claudia. They reside near Houston, Texas.

about young endeavors

Young Endeavors is the preaching and resource ministry of Thomas Young. Through Young Endeavors, Thomas has produced Bible study resources used by groups and churches. Also available are "Accelerate" devotional cd's, Bible study books, and other materials. These materials are widely used because of

their sound Biblical content and powerful applications to our lives.

It is the desire of Thomas and Young Endeavors to continue to emphasize the need for Christians to know the truths of God's Word—and particularly the basic doctrines of the Christian faith.

To schedule Thomas or to order materials:

Go online to:

www.youngendeavors.org or www.thomasyoung.com

Or write to:

YOUNG ENDEAVORS

The Ministry with Thomas
Young

314 Morton Ave. Suite #11

Richmond, Texas 77469

Or call:

281-341-1230

to order more books

If God has used this book to touch your life, you may want to give copies to family and friends who are serious about following Christ. The book is also designed for small groups. The questions at the end of each chapter stimulate terrific discussions.

Discount Information

1 book $15.99 each

2-9 $14.99 each

10-24 $13.99 each

25-100 $11.99 each

Shipping

1 book: $4

2-24 books: $2/each

25-100 books: $1/each

Over 100-call 281-341-1230

To Order

By phone: Call 281-341-1230

On the web. www.thomasyoung.com

By mail: YOUNG ENDEAVORS

314 Morton Ave. Suite #11

Richmond, TX 77469

Credit cards accepted online. Checks accepted by mail.

For other Books and Bible Study Resources, visit

www.youngendeavors.org

Notes

Notes